Russell Barr

VANTASTIC

&

LOBSTER

OBERON BOOKS
LONDON

First published in 2009 by Oberon Books Ltd
521 Caledonian Road, London N7 9RH
Tel: 020 7607 3637 / Fax: 020 7607 3629
e-mail: info@oberonbooks.com
www.oberonbooks.com

A catalogue record for this book is available from the British
Library.

ISBN: 978-1-84002-980-2

Cover photograph: Getty Images. Cover design by Bob Karper.

Printed in Great Britain by CPI Antony Rowe, Chippenham.

Contents

The writer would like to thank the following for their continued support:

Jess Alford, Jim and Eleanor Barr, Ronald and Marjory Barr, Jonathan Best, Evie Cameron, Max Stafford Clark, Graham Crowley, Pearce Crowley, Robin Crowley, Sally Crowley, Tommy and Jean Cuthbertson, Garry Everett at Homotopia, Henrietta Faire, Thomas Faire, Stella Feehily, Linda Gamble, Glenn and Sally Goodey, Richard E Grant, Charlotte Gwinner, Sir David Hare, Lena Headey, Rachel Hopkin, Nicholas Hytner, G. Hollerin, John Hutton, Gareth James, Dr Dominic Johnson, Bob Karper, Lois Keidan at the Live Art Development Agency, Gerard Kelly Davie Elder, Kent Lawson, Liz Littlewood and Arts Council England, Sandy and Sheila Livingstone, Zoe Livingstone, Robin and Hazel Lumsden, Kirsten Matthew, Andrew John McClelland, Donovan Munitich, Shane Murphy, Yve Newbold, Julie Parker, Tim Plester, Queer up North, Alan Rickman, St John Donald, Carol Tambor, Peter Todd, Zoe Tossell, Tom Stoppard, Barnaby Welch, Richard Wilson, Ruth Young, everyone at Oval House Theatre.

This book is dedicated to the memory of my Grandmothers,
Nan McLees and Charlotte Barr.

Vantastic and *Lobster* were first performed at the Oval House Theatre on 17 November 2009, with the following cast:

VANTASTIC
PAM, Eileen Nicholas
PETER, Richard Syms
DODDIE, Richard Flood
SCRATCHIT, Clare Grogan
BOY, Leo Richardson

LOBSTER
CHATTY, Eileen Nicholas
TOBIAS, Richard Flood
BOY, Leo Richardson

Written by Russell Barr
Produced by Natasha Davis in collaboration with the Oval House

Director Luke Kernaghan
Designer Peter Todd
Lighting Designer Marty Langthorne
Composer Felix Faire
Assistant Director Kenneth O' Toole

VANTASTIC

Characters

PAM
PETER
DODDIE
SCRATCHIT
BOY

We see two caravans on a patch of turf.

A BOY appears. Eighteen. Handsome. He is wearing a tracksuit. He enters one of the caravans, and picks up a photograph.

He looks at it for some time. He takes it out its frame, and puts it in his pocket.

The BOY exits the caravan, leaving the door open.

PAM enters the caravan. She is wearing a tracksuit.

The / symbol indicates when the next character should start talking.

PAM: Peter? / Peter?

PETER: Yes?

PAM: Would you answer me please / Peter?

PETER: What is it?

PAM: What on earth is the door to the New Hampshire doing open?

PETER: (*Shouting from the car.*) I don't know Pam.

PAM: You left it open Peter.

PETER: (*Still shouting from the car.*) I did not leave / it open.

PAM: Do not deny it. This is a brand new, 'New Hampshire' caravan. Seventy thousand pounds worth. Brand new leather sofa. Brand new 'American style fridge'. Brand new beds. Brand new loo. Everything brand new. And you leave the door open. You leave the door of a brand new, 'New Hampshire' caravan open? / What are you thinking?

PETER: (*Still shouting from the car.*) I DID NOT LEAVE THE BLOODY DOOR OPEN. I DID NOT LEAVE IT OPEN PAM!

PETER holds his chest.

Pause.

PETER enters the caravan. He is wearing a tracksuit, he carries a stuffed collie cross (Shaggy).

PAM: Oh Peter. Isn't this super?

PETER: What is?

PAM: Isn't this super?

PETER: What is?

PAM: The brand new 'New Hampshire'.

PETER: Yes, Pam.

PAM: Would you not agree that it's super?

PETER: / Yes, super.

PAM: I never thought I would like the American style. But I really admire it. I think it's a very clever investment. Our last thirty thousand. My idea. Do you think it's better than the Chalet?

PETER: Much.

PAM: You think it's better than the Chalet?

PETER: Much better than / the Chalet.

PAM: The Chalet was your idea.
Dip Shaggy. He is quite a hot dog.

PETER: Shaggy was dipped not twenty minutes ago. At that Little Chef.

PAM: He might die due to heat exhaustion. And if he did die, whose fault would that be? Peter?

PETER: Not mine Pam. Not mine.

PETER stands holding Shaggy. He does nothing.

PAM: Get out and dip Shaggy. Remember, Hot Dogs Kill!

There is a pause, PETER does not move.

PETER: What do you suggest I dip Shaggy in?

PAM: In the bucket. Dip Shaggy in the bucket. The bucket outside the 'New Hampshire' caravan.

PETER: The yellow / bucket?

PAM: Are you special needs Peter?

PETER exits the caravan.

There is a pause. PAM begins to deal with the tupperwares.

She takes a knife out the drawer. She looks at it.

(*Still looking at the knife.*) Do you not think it's a shame about the Little Chefs?

PETER: Sorry?

PAM: The Little Chefs. Do you not think it's / a shame?

PETER: Well Pam that's the way the cookie crumbles.

PAM: Free refills and a nice clean toilet at the Little Chefs.

PETER: Mmmmm.

PAM: Have you had your Warfarin Peter?

PETER: No. Looking forward to seeing your daughter?

PAM: I don't look forward to anything anymore.

PETER: Right. Not optimistic.

PAM: No. Not anymore.

PETER: Well, that's a shame.

PAM: Fucking hell.

PETER: What?

PAM: You have left the lobster in Aberystwyth.

PETER: You never told me / to bring the lobster.

PAM: (*Angry.*) We're not money bags you know. What a bloody waste of a lobster. Where the hell's Shaggy?

PETER: Oh, let him have a bit / of fresh air, and a little run around.

PAM: Please, please, please would you take your Warfarin.

PETER: Where are they?

PAM: I don't know. I am not your carer Peter. Get Shaggy in.

PETER goes to exit the caravan. He notices the picture is gone.

PETER: The photograph has gone.

PAM: What?

PETER: The picture of us Martin / with us.

PAM: Get out Peter and get Shaggy.

DODDIE is sat on his own.

SCRATCHIT enters. She is carrying a large bag full of medicine.

SCRATCHIT: Do you know who you remind me of?

DODDIE: Who?

SCRATCHIT: Pierce Brosnan.

DODDIE: Oh thanks very much.

SCRATCHIT: You look like a cross between Pierce Brosnan and Ken Dodd.

DODDIE: Oh Jesus. Piss off.

SCRATCHIT: Do you know what would be a good name for you.

DODDIE: (*With contempt.*) Tell me.

SCRATCHIT: Doddie.

DODDIE: Good luck with that.

SCRATCHIT: I want a cuddle.

DODDIE: What?

SCRATCHIT: I want a cuddle.

DODDIE: No.

SCRATCHIT: I want a cuddle. / Give me a cuddle now.

DODDIE: No. Piss off.

SCRATCHIT: I am feeling very vulnerable. / Cuddle. Now!

DODDIE: What is in that bag?

SCRATCHIT: It's a secret.

DODDIE: (*Grabbing the bag.*) Show me what is in the bag.

SCRATCHIT: No.

DODDIE: What's all this for?

SCRATCHIT: Early menopause.

DODDIE: I thought the doctor's wouldn't / give you any medicine?

SCRATCHIT: I am now. Officially. Self. Medicating.

DODDIE: Right.

SCRATCHIT: I bought them off eBay.

DODDIE: You have got to be joking. Is that wise?

SCRATCHIT: Do not CUNTING question me. It's my business. My fucking menopause. / I AM SELF MEDICATING.

DODDIE: Have you got something there that helps with your anger?

SCRATCHIT: FUCK OFF DODDIE.

DODDIE: Stop swearing.

SCRATCHIT: It's one of the symptoms

DODDIE: That's a poor excuse.

SCRATCHIT: I'm warning you?

DODDIE: 'T-bomb two, maximum strength testosterone'. / This is for body builders.

SCRATCHIT: Do you love me? Do you love me.

DODDIE: What?

SCRATCHIT: I was just wondering if you loved me?

DODDIE: Right.

SCRATCHIT: It's very important for me to know. With my current condition.

DODDIE: No.

SCRATCHIT: You said you did last week.

DODDIE: Did I?

SCRATCHIT: Last week you said you truly loved me.

DODDIE: Was I pissed?

SCRATCHIT: Love me now?

DODDIE: (*Lifting a box.*) Android-10?

SCRATCHIT: Love me Pip?

DODDIE: / Can I have a go?

SCRATCHIT: Love me, love me, love me, / love me Pip?

DODDIE: Stop that. Stop it now.

SCRATCHIT: Now. Love me now. I want you to love me now!

DODDIE: My therapist Mrs Taylor would say that was inappropriate.

SCRATCHIT: Right then. The middle aged testosterone victim is having a marvellous / big testosterone day.

SCRATCHIT takes some pills.

DODDIE is examining the medicines.

DODDIE: (*Looking at more medicine.*) What about taking some 'NuvaRing', cheer you up?

SCRATCHIT: That's for my vagina.

There is a pause.

What about the orgy?

DODDIE: What are you talking about?

SCRATCHIT: What about the orgy.

DODDIE: What about it?

SCRATCHIT: What about the orgy?

DODDIE: What about it.

SCRATCHIT: You shat the sofa.

DODDIE: That's right.

SCRATCHIT: You shat on the white Ikea sofa.

DODDIE: Yes.

SCRATCHIT: You stood in the toilet.

DODDIE: Yes.

SCRATCHIT: And were you embarrassed?

DODDIE: Yes. I looked in the mirror and laughed.

SCRATCHIT: And then what happened Doddie?

DODDIE: Then I went back for more.

SCRATCHIT: You got finished off. Didn't you Doddie.

DODDIE: No. I went home. Enough of the Doddie's now.

SCRATCHIT: You smelt of jobbies Doddie.

DODDIE: Yes.

SCRATCHIT: Sad isn't it? And did anyone touch you Doddie?

DODDIE: Nope.

SCRATCHIT: Who would Doddie?

DODDIE: Exactly. Who would. I stood there watching. The best bit is getting accepted. It all goes downhill after that. The loneliness is palpable.

SCRATCHIT: The loneliness?

DODDIE: Yes. It's palpable. You have to fill the void.

SCRATCHIT: The untouchable. Filling the void. You're a dirty boy. But I love you.

DODDIE: I love you too.

SCRATCHIT: Yes?

DODDIE kisses SCRATCHIT. It is the kiss of lovers.

DODDIE: Does that make you feel better?

SCRATCHIT: Yes. Much.

The BOY we saw earlier is standing in the doorway to the 'New Hampshire'. He is holding the stuffed dog. PETER is reading the Telegraph.

PAM: Oh Jesus. Give me the dog. Give me the dog you horrible little fart. GIVE. ME. THE. DOG. GIVE. ME. SHAGGY.

The BOY is still holding on to Shaggy, PETER is reading the Daily Telegraph.

Peter do / something.

PETER: What do you want me to do Pam?

PAM: Put down the newspaper and get Shaggy, he is crushing the bloody thing to death. Shaggy is panting now.

PETER: I don't see him panting.

PAM: He is. He's internally panting.

PETER: Internally panting? What the hell does that mean. Internally panting.

PAM: He's foreign.

PETER: Shaggy is foreign?

PAM: The boy, you arsehole. The boy is / foreign?

PETER: (*To the BOY.*) Are you foreign son?

The BOY says nothing.

(*Speaking slowly.*) Where. Are. / You. From?

PAM: Oh this is absolutely fucking useless.

PETER: Answer the question son. Are you foreign?
Are you Polish? Are you seeking asylum?
Are you a gypsy? / Are you gypsy?

PAM is now hysterical.

PAM: HE'S NOT A FUCKING GYPSY. GIVE ME BACK
MY FUCKING DOG. GIVE ME BACK SHAGGY. /
GIVE ME THE FUCKING DOG.

PETER: Listen, you little bastard. Put Shaggy down now.

The BOY does nothing.

Speak when you're spoken to. Come on. Are. You. /
Gypsy?

PAM: HE'S NOT GYPSY!!!!

PETER: Welsh?

PAM: Do you think?

PAM begins to warm her lips up.

(*Pointing at the little BOY.*) Cymraeg?

The BOY puts the dog down.

PETER: There's a good boy.

PETER continues to read the Daily Telegraph.

PAM: (*Still pointing.*) Cymraeg?

The BOY does not respond. He is now smiling.

PETER: Try a different phrase?

PAM: I am just keeping things simple.
Beth ydy'ch / enw chi?

PETER: Super job Pamela, super job.

PAM: Don't patronise me, Peter.

PAM: Dwi'n aros ym Mythonood Gwyliau Cwmtawe – mae'n wych. Welsh is such a / lovely language.

PETER: You have just told him that you are staying in the Swansea Valley Holiday Cottages / and they're great.

PAM: Don't be stupid Peter.

PETER: You have.

PAM: You know my feelings on South Wales.

The BOY reaches out his hand.

PETER: What is he doing.

PAM: I don't know.

PETER: Put your hand down. Now.

The BOY moves towards PAM.

PAM: Oh Jesus. Is he going to rape me?

PETER: Don't be ridiculous Pam.

The BOY moves towards PAM. He touches PAM's face.

He touched your face.

PAM: Finger on the pulse Peter.

PETER: How weird.

PAM: Weird.

PETER: Yes weird?

The BOY keeps his hand on PAM's face.

That's enough now.

The BOY does not move.

Take your hand off my wife.

The BOY does not move.

Take your hands off my wife you / little shit.

(*Ushering the BOY out of the caravan.*) Thank you very much. Out you go. We have had enough of you now.

There is a pause. PETER continues to read the Daily Telegraph. *The BOY appears at the window above PETER's head. He knocks on the window. PETER gets a fright.*

Oh bloody hell!

PAM: (*To the BOY.*) Bugger off.

The BOY does the V sign.

Peter, would you do something?

PETER: I'm not quite sure what you expect me to do.

PAM: Get rid of him.

The BOY continues to do the V sign.

And why are you reading the *Daily Telegraph*?

PETER: I wanted a change. / I wanted a change.

PAM: That is a very expensive newspaper. Why did you not buy *The Times*?

PETER: I wanted a change.

PAM: You save ten pence buying *The Times* Peter. It is very, very extravagant behaviour.

The BOY continues to do the V sign.

Bugger off! What's 'go away', in Welsh? Spwng dorth. Spwng dorth.

PAM starts shouting at the BOY. The BOY disappears. There is a pause.

PETER: You just shouted 'Spunk loaf' at that boy.

PAM: Don't be ridiculous.

PETER: You did. You shouted 'spunk loaf'.

A BOY appears at the door of the 'New Hampshire' caravan. He is carrying a bottle of testosterone pills.

SCRATCHIT: Hand over the pills.

The BOY does nothing.

GIVE. ME. THE. TESTOSTERONE.

The BOY does nothing.

Please can you help me here?

DODDIE: What do you want me / to do?

SCRATCHIT: I am beginning to panic. Get the pills off him.

DODDIE: Give me the pills? Give me the pills.

The BOY does nothing.

Hand over the pills you little shite.

The BOY does nothing.

SCRATCHIT: GIVE ME THE PILLS, GIVE ME THE FUCKING PILLS, / YOU FUCKING LITTLE CUNT.

SCRATCHIT gets the pills. DODDIE pulls SCRATCHIT off the BOY.

DODDIE: OK Scratchit. That's enough.

The BOY says nothing.

SCRATCHIT and the BOY look at each other. There is a pause. SCRATCHIT holds the pills close to her chest. There is a long pause. The BOY looks tenderly at DODDIE and SCRATCHIT.

SCRATCHIT: Innocent little face.

DODDIE: Yes.

SCRATCHIT: Surprising.

DODDIE: Yes. Very. Especially these days. In this world.

SCRATCHIT: Lucky.

DODDIE: Yes. Wish I was like that.

The BOY reaches out and touches SCRATCHIT's face.

SCRATCHIT: Jesus. Is he going to rape me?

DODDIE: Don't be ridiculous.

BOY: Spwng dorth.

SCRATCHIT: What?

BOY: Spwng dorth.

DODDIE: What language is that.

BOY: Spwng dorth.

SCRATCHIT: Welsh.

BOY: Spwng dorth.

DODDIE: Well what does it mean?

BOY: Spwng dorth.

SCRATCHIT: I don't know. (*Pointing at the boy.*) Siared Cymraeg?

The BOY smiles.

BOY: Spwng dorth. Spwng dorth.

The BOY smiles again.

Spwng dorth.

The BOY smiles. There is a pause.

Spwng dorth.

DODDIE: Do you think he has Asperger's?

BOY: Spwng dorth. Spwng dorth. Spwng dorth. Spwng dorth.

DODDIE: Is that all you can say?

BOY: Spwng dorth. Spwng dorth.

SCRATCHIT: Get rid of him.

DODDIE: Thank you. Bugger off. That's enough now.

BOY: SPWNG DORTH.

DODDIE ushers the BOY out of the caravan.

DODDIE: What a charming little creature he was. Attractive though.

SCRATCHIT: Paedophile.

DODDIE: He's a teenager.

SCRATCHIT: You don't realise what you've got. You boys are lucky. You're never lonely.

The BOY does the V sign at the window.

FUCK OFF.

DODDIE: You're all resentful now.

SCRATCHIT: Time for some more pills I think.

DODDIE: Horny little fucker. I would love to fuck him bareback.

There is a pause. DODDIE and the BOY wink at each other.

SCRATCHIT: You certainly can't behave like that if we get married.

DODDIE: We're getting married?

SCRATCHIT: Yes. You promised. You said you loved me, and that we were getting married.

DODDIE: Maybe I might marry that boy instead.

SCRATCHIT: Fuck you Doddie.

SCRATCHIT exits the caravan. There is a pause.

DODDIE is sat on his own. A mobile telephone goes off. He checks the message. It is a video of two people having sex.

He plays the video again.

The BOY appears at the door of the caravan.

BOY: What are you looking at?

DODDIE: Oh you can speak then.

BOY: Spwng Dorth.

DODDIE: What does it mean.

BOY: Spunk loaf I think.

DODDIE: Charming.

BOY: What are you looking at.

DODDIE: Nothing.

BOY: That's a lie. That's a lie.

DODDIE: Excuse me?

BOY: I saw you looking at something on your phone.

DODDIE: It was nothing. I wasn't looking at anything.

BOY: That's a lie.

DODDIE: Stop saying that.

BOY: Why?
I like it here.

DODDIE: It's horrible.

BOY: Like seeing the families. Through the windows.

DODDIE: Right. Yes.

BOY: I like seeing them all together. The twinkling lights.

There is a pause. The BOY stares at DODDIE.

DODDIE: What are you staring at?

BOY: You. I want to see what you were looking at. On your phone.

DODDIE: It's rude.

BOY: I'm sure I can handle it.

DODDIE: It's very rude.

BOY: Just let me see.

DODDIE plays the video on his phone of the brothers.

Who are they?

DODDIE: Just boys.

BOY: Where did you meet them?

DODDIE: I've never met them. They are off the internet.

BOY: Horny.

DODDIE looks at the BOY.

DODDIE: They are twins.

BOY: Really?

DODDIE: The two boys. Identical twins.

BOY: Fuck.

DODDIE: They fuck each other all the time. They want me to watch. And then two of us can fuck the passive brother.

BOY: Passive?

DODDIE: You know. Passive. Active. Or versatile.

BOY: Nope.

DODDIE: Oh it's too hard to explain.

BOY: Are you going to fuck them?

DODDIE: Don't think so. My therapist, Mrs Taylor, thinks that fucking identical twins is a bit inappropriate.

BOY: It sounds horny.

DODDIE: Right.

BOY: Fucking horny.

The BOY grabs DODDIE and kisses him hard. They kiss for some time.

DODDIE pulls away.

DODDIE: How old are you?

BOY: Fifteen.

DODDIE: Right.

The BOY kisses DODDIE again. They kiss for some time. SCRATCHIT looks through the window.

BOY: Take your top off.

DODDIE: Yeah?

BOY: Yes. Take your top off.

DODDIE stands up. He takes his vest off.

The BOY kisses DODDIE again.

Nice pecs Mr.

The BOY rubs DODDIE's chest.

DODDIE: No pecs, no sex. Eh Mr?

BOY: What?

DODDIE: Never mind.

BOY: Show me your cock. You horny fuck.

DODDIE: I have a broken frenulum.

BOY: A what.

DODDIE: The bit of skin that joins the head to the shaft, I'm having a bit of trouble with it.

BOY: I don't mind.

DODDIE: I do.

BOY: I want to see your cock.

DODDIE: Not with a broken frenulum you don't. Where's your Mum?

BOY: She's dead.

DODDIE: Right. Sorry.

BOY: Cancer. Riddled with it.

DODDIE: And your Father.

BOY: Also dead. Brutally murdered.

DODDIE: Brothers?

BOY: Nope.

DODDIE: Sisters?

BOY: Nope.

DODDIE: You're a little orphan.

BOY: Yes. I'd like a family.

DODDIE: Must be sad. To be on your own. Handsome little orphan.

DODDIE kisses him on the head. There is a pause.

BOY: Maybe you could be my new boyfriend?

PAM and PETER are in their caravan.

PAM: Haliad hallt.

PETER: I don't know that one.

PAM: Welsh for Salty wank.

PETER: Thank you Pam.

PAM: Jini Ffernac.

PETER: That is enough.

PAM: Tampon. That means tampon.

PETER: Thank you.

PAM: You are a big Sioncen Peter.

PETER: What?

PAM: You're a big vagina, / Peter.

PETER: Thank you very much. That's bloody charming.

PAM: What about the jewellery business?

PETER: Why are you bringing that up now?

PAM: Well it wasn't me selling jewellery shops / willy-nilly.

PETER: I don't want to / talk about it.

PAM: Then you panicked and we moved to a horrible seventies council estate in East Kilbride. Awful. / Really ghastly.

PETER: You were the one that panicked Pam. / You're the panicker.

PAM: Panic? It is not in MY nature to / panic.

PETER: It wasn't a council estate anyway.

PAM: Oh shut up.

PETER: It was a housing estate Pamela. We weren't living / on a council estate.

PAM: Panic? What kind of a word is / that to use?

PETER: I paid for that house. You did you panicked.

PAM: Stop saying that. / It's ridiculous.

PETER: I sold the jewellery shops and you panicked.

PAM: Stop saying panicked. / Stop it.

PETER: Fine. We all know where this leads.

PAM: Oh do we now?

PETER: Yes we do.

PAM: Then there was that bloody Leisure Centre. I wanted a farm Peter. For the children. Are you not going to say anything?

PETER: No.

PAM: Nothing.

PETER: Nothing.

PAM: Nothing at all.

PETER: Nope. / Nothing.

PAM: A Leisure Centre Peter? What kind of a bonkers idea was that?

PETER does not respond. PAM comes very close to PETER.

(*Speaking in a childish voice.*) Do you not remember / Peter? Do you not remember buying the Leisure Centre?

PETER: Of course I bloody well do Pam.

PAM: What the hell were you thinking?

PETER: I thought the children / would like it.

PAM: That's a very stupid statement.

PETER: I thought it was the best option / for the children.

PAM: You had us living in the conference suite.

PETER: I thought / it was best for the children.

PAM: Well, its baffling isn't it? Absolutely baffling. I had a baby mongol Peter. You cannot put a mongol / in a Conference Suite.

PETER: Martin had a cot.

PAM: The Mongol had a cot in a Conference Suite. A cot in a bloody Conference Suite. Post natal depression in a Conference Suite. What were you thinking?

PETER: (*Defiant.*) I liked the Leisure Centre Pam. I liked it.

PAM: What about the staff?

PETER: What about them.

PAM: They were all completely out of control.

PETER: That's the way the cookie crumbles Pam.

PAM: You had the managing skill of a goldfish Peter. The swimming pool attendant was constantly pissed.

PETER: Yes. David was a problem.

PAM: He should have been fired Peter. I am sure that crèche lady was a convicted paedophile.

PETER: Well, you could have helped.

PAM: I HAD A BABY MONGOL. WE WERE LIVING IN A CONFERENCE SUITE. / FUCKING HELL.

PAM throws a spoon at PETER.

PETER: You could have done something Pam.

PAM: A fucking conference suite.

The BOY appears at the window again, doing the V sign. PAM loses it, she punches the side of the caravan.

FUCK OFF. GO ON FUCK OFF. YOU LITTLE CUNT.

PETER: That is enough.

PAM: Oh, do you really think so.

PETER: Yes I do. Stop this now. You are really wound up. You need to wind down.

PAM: I am really wound up am I?

PETER: Yes you need / to wind down.

PAM: The oracle has spoken, I need to fucking / wind down.

PETER: Stop it Pam. / You've stepped over the line.

PAM: Oooooooh. Peter's taking control.

PETER: Please Pam. / That is enough.

PAM: (*Taking the paper out PETER's hand.*) No Peter, I will tell you when I have had enough. You will not tell me. Is that clear?

PETER says nothing.

Answer the question.

PETER says nothing.

She crushes up the Daily Telegraph *and throws it on to the floor. There is a stand off. PETER looks scared.*

Is. That. Clear.

PETER: Yes Pam. It. Is. Clear.

PAM: You insolent little fucker.

He reaches down to the floor to pick up the newspaper.

Leave it.

He reaches again.

Leave the fucking *Telegraph.*

PETER looks pathetic. He is sitting. PAM is standing over him. They both know what is going to happen.

(*Calmly.*) A Conference Suite. I had a baby, and we were living in a Conference Suite. A Conference Suite. With a fucking Mongol.

PAM punches PETER in the face. She walks over to the kitchen area, and continues preparing the dinner.

PETER is crying. He reaches down for the newspaper, and begins to flatten it out, and continues reading. He has blood dripping down his face.

DODDIE and SCRATCHIT are in their caravan.

DODDIE: How long has Shaggy been stuffed for?

SCRATCHIT: Since 1973. She had an attachment.

DODDIE: An attachment?

SCRATCHIT: Yes. She had an unusually close attachment to Shaggy. Shaggy became the son she never had.

DODDIE: And you don't think that's a bit fucked.

SCRATCHIT: What about me?

DODDIE: What about you?

SCRATCHIT: What about me?

DODDIE: What about you?

SCRATCHIT: What about me?

DODDIE: What about you?

SCRATCHIT: I do love you.

DODDIE: Yes?

SCRATCHIT: I'm not sure quite what I would do without you.

DODDIE: Me too.

SCRATCHIT: We are like a little family.

DODDIE: Yes.

SCRATCHIT: Who's the Mummy?

DODDIE: I don't know.

SCRATCHIT: Who's the Daddy?

DODDIE: I don't know.

SCRATCHIT: You don't know?

DODDIE: I think you should go and hang out with your brother.

SCRATCHIT: Martin?

DODDIE: Yes. Go and hang out with the mongol. Maybe he will be your friend.

SCRATCHIT: I never knew what to say to Martin.

DODDIE: I liked the autistic ones better than the spastics, especially Margarine Michelle. She ate handfuls of margarine out of the fridge. We had to padlock it twice. Strong little Jewish fucker.

SCRATCHIT: They have great strength the Jews. Didn't we have a super mini-break at Auschwitz.

DODDIE: We had a huge fight in Auschwitz and you called me a sex tourist.

SCRATCHIT: I don't / remember that.

DODDIE: Outside Birkenau. You called me a sex tourist. How can one be a sex tourist in Auschwitz?

SCRATCHIT: I saw you kiss that boy. You dirty fuck.

There is a pause.

DODDIE: It's like Auschwitz here.

SCRATCHIT: What?

DODDIE: The whole place is surrounded in barbed wire. It's like they want to keep you in.

SCRATCHIT: Locked away?

DODDIE: Yeah.

SCRATCHIT: I rather like it.

DODDIE: To be locked away?

SCRATCHIT: It is better than the world.

DODDIE: You think?

SCRATCHIT: I am here. With you. I don't need anything else. And you don't need that boy.

Pause.

DODDIE: You don't think it's odd that I am totally surrounded by ladies that are older / than me?

SCRATCHIT: Am I included in that?

DODDIE: Fuck yes. I am totally surrounded by middle aged, single women.

SCRATCHIT says nothing.

All you single, childless, middle aged people are fucking bonkers.

SCRATCHIT: Stop it.

DODDIE: The lesbians that don't have children are all in mental homes.

SCRATCHIT: What?

DODDIE: All those single lesbians are in mental homes.

SCRATCHIT: You sound like a misogynist.

DODDIE: Bring it back. Bring back a good dose of seventies, homosexual misogyny.

SCRATCHIT: Stop this. / It's fucking ridiculous.

DODDIE: I'm serious. I have had it.

SCRATCHIT: I've been very good to you. I've been a very good supportive friend.

DODDIE: What about Frankie?

SCRATCHIT: She wanted to have your baby.

DODDIE: Yeah. And I was stupid enough to take her seriously.

SCRATCHIT: Stop this.

DODDIE: You asked if I would adopt a child with you.

SCRATCHIT: And you said yes.

DODDIE: Fucking lucky the Catholic Adoption Agency said no then, wasn't it. That boy is an orphan.

SCRATCHIT: That's sad.

DODDIE: I don't think so. It means he is very available.

PAM is on her own.

After a while PETER enters.

PAM: Have you taken the Warfarin?

PETER: Christ. No.

PAM: Oh, for God's sake Peter. I do not want you dying on us.

PETER: I'll take the pill.

PAM: If you have a bloody heart attack here. It's curtains.
There's not a hospital for miles.

PETER: Where did you say the pills were?

PAM: I have warned you about this. In the volvo. In the glove
compartment of the toilet-blue volvo.

PETER stands up once again. He looks tired. He exits the caravan.

Do you want curry or stew for your tea.

DODDIE and SCRATCHIT are in their caravan.

DODDIE: Do you really think you would be a fit mother?

SCRATCHIT: Yes.

DODDIE: Well I don't think you're up to it.

SCRATCHIT: You'd help. If I did adopt.

DODDIE: No I wouldn't.

SCRATCHIT: You promised.

DODDIE: I should never have offered.

SCRATCHIT: You can't expect me to do this on my own.

There is a pause.

DODDIE: I made her have an abortion.

SCRATCHIT: Who?

DODDIE: Frankie.

SCRATCHIT: Whose baby was it?

DODDIE: Mine.

SCRATCHIT: I thought you / said no.

DODDIE: I lied. We did the turkey baster.

SCRATCHIT: Why didn't you have sexual intercourse.

DODDIE: I could do it with that lesbian. But not her.

SCRATCHIT: Oh.

DODDIE: She had a face like a burst couch.

Pause.

She had to sit on a plastic sheet for three days.

SCRATCHIT: Right.

DODDIE: Each day bits of it came out.

SCRATCHIT: Why did you do it?

DODDIE: I loved her.

SCRATCHIT: And now you love me.

DODDIE: Did I say that?

SCRATCHIT: Yes.

DODDIE: Right.

SCRATCHIT: I am jealous.

DODDIE: Of what?

SCRATCHIT: That you did it with her and not with me. It should have been me.

Pause.

Please Doddie, have a baby with me.

PAM enters DODDIE and SCRATCHIT's caravan.

PAM: Hello. Hello.

SCRATCHIT: Oh hello.

PAM: How are you dear.

SCRATCHIT: Yes. Uhu. Fine.

PAM: Would you like a curry or stew for your tea?

Pause.

What's that on your face Petronella?

SCRATCHIT: What?

PAM: That stuff. All over your face. What is it?

SCRATCHIT: What are you talking about?

PAM: Spread all over your face.

SCRATCHIT: It's make up. It's bloody make up.

PAM: Oh dearie me.
  You look like a camel chewing a toffee.

DODDIE: She is going through the early menopause.

SCRATCHIT: For fuck's sake.

PAM: Oh bloody marvellous.

SCRATCHIT: It wasn't / planned Mum.

PAM: This is a bit of a bombshell. So we are absolutely
  screwed for grandchildren?

SCRATCHIT: Well. Yes.

PAM: Is this attention seeking?

SCRATCHIT: / What?

PAM: Are you seeking attention?

SCRATCHIT: No.

PAM: Well it seems very convenient.

SCRATCHIT: Convenient?

PAM: Your Mother never had a menopause.

SCRATCHIT: Well you're lucky.

PAM: It's a terrible disappointment.

SCRATCHIT: I have found it / really hard.

PAM: What are the other symptoms?

SCRATCHIT: I don't really want to / talk about it.

PAM: Teach Mummy and your wee Boyfriend about the
  menopause.

SCRATCHIT: Irregular periods. Bladder control problems. Gastrointestinal distress and nausea. Bloating. Hair loss. Facial hair. Changes in body odour. / Dry mouth and other oral symptoms.

PAM: Oh marvellous. I'm going to end up with a fat, bearded stinking, incontinent lump of a daughter. Just what I always wanted. You always were my little fatty.

PAM pinches SCRATCHIT's cheek.

DODDIE: Vaginal atrophy.

SCRATCHIT: Shut up / Doddie?

PAM: Vaginal atrophy?

DODDIE: That's one of the / other symptoms.

PAM: What is it?

DODDIE: Dry fanny.

PAM: I better go and tell your Father the good news. I am sure he will be thrilled. She always was my little fatty.
Now, do come and see the 'New Hampshire'. It's marvellous. We have a brand new American-style fridge-freezer with built-in ice-maker.

PAM exits the caravan.

Do you want curry or stew for your tea?

PETER is brushing Shaggy.

PETER: Don't you have a lovely healthy coat Shaggy poo.

PAM enters the caravan.

PAM: Is my Shaggy asleep?

PETER: Yes.

PAM: Did you change his nappy?

PETER: Yes.

PAM: Have you taken the Warfarin?

PETER: Yes.

PAM: Were they in the glove compartment of the toilet-blue / volvo?

PETER: Yes.

PAM: I told you so.

There is a pause.

I could have been something, Peter.

PETER: What are you talking about now?

PAM: I could have been something.

PETER: Right.

PAM: I could have been something. What is so difficult about that sentence?

PETER: Nothing. Nothing's difficult.

PAM: Well, when you look at it, in black and white. It's quite / sad.

PETER: It wasn't possible Pam.

PAM: Because of Beryl.

PETER: Yes.

PAM: Beryl, made it not possible.

PETER: Mmmm.

PAM: Your Mother. Beryl. You feel no regret.

PETER: Sorry?

PAM: That your mother stopped me living. She made me keep Martin. She said it was wrong.

PETER: You could have stood up to her.

PAM: What?

PETER: You heard me. You could have stood up / to her.

PAM: No, Peter.

PETER: That's the way the cookie crumbles Pam.

PAM: Fuck the cookie. Fuck the fucking cookie.

> *There is a pause. PAM is upset.*

> *PAM goes to the kitchen. She takes a knife out of the drawer. She gently takes it down the side of her face. It does not cut her. She does it over and over again. PETER does nothing. PAM does not cut herself.*

> *PETER rises. He goes over to PAM and takes the knife out of her hand.*

> *He kisses the blade of the knife.*

> *The both stare at each other.*

Your daughter is going through the early menopause. Another fucking disappointment. Apparently she has a dry fanny.

PETER: Don't be foul Pam.

> *PAM is left on her own. She is stroking Shaggy.*

PAM: Lovely dog. Don't you have a super glossy coat. My lovely Shaggy. I love you. You are all I have left.

> *PAM kisses Shaggy.*

BOY: Hello blood.

PAM: Oh hello. Blood?

BOY: Yeah. You're my blood.

PAM: Right. Yes. Hello blood.

BOY: Pow Pow blood.

PAM: Yeah. Pow pow.

BOY: Fucking / sweet.

PAM: Where's your mother?

BOY: Dead.

PAM: Your Father.

BOY: Never met him.

PAM: You're not Welsh.

BOY: Cancer.

PAM: That's very disappointing.

BOY: She died quickly.

The BOY smiles. Pause.

You're hot missus.

PAM: Sorry.

BOY: You're fucking hot.

PAM: Right. Yes.

BOY: I wanna taste your old pumplex.

PAM: Pumplex?

BOY: Yeah blood.

PAM: What's a pumplex?

BOY: Fanny innit. I wanna taste your old cunt.

PAM: Super.

BOY: You're bang on it.

PAM: Bang on what?

BOY: You wanna let a young boy fuck you?

PAM: Well. Yes. / Why not.

BOY: Fucking hot. I wanna bang you hard.

PAM: You sure you can handle it.

BOY: I'm sure I can handle it. You are bare rude blood.

PAM: I am bare rude. Super. Come on bang me hard. Blood.

BOY: Sweet.

PAM: I still have my juices.

BOY: Fucking sweet.

PAM: Unlike my dried up daughter.

The BOY clicks his fingers, in the rapper style.

There is a pause.

BOY: Then will you be my Granny?

PAM: What?

BOY: After I fuck you. Will you be my Granny?

PAM: Eh?

BOY: I really want a Granny.

PAM: I am afraid I wouldn't make a very good Granny.

BOY: You wouldn't like a sweet little Grandson?

PAM: Like you.

BOY: Yes like me.

PAM: Which would you rather?

BOY: What?

PAM: Fuck or a Granny?

BOY: Granny please.

PAM: /Shame.

BOY: You could just pretend.

PAM: Right.

BOY: Hello Granny.

PAM: Right. Hello.

BOY: Can I have a cuddle?

PAM: Sorry?

BOY: That's what Grannies do. They cuddle. / I love you Granny.

PAM: This is stupid.

BOY: No it's not. You're my Granny. Cuddle me.

PAM: Get out.

BOY: Please Granny give me a cuddle.

PAM: Would you like to kiss my Shaggy?

BOY: Fuck no.

PAM: Well get out then.

BOY: Cuddle NOW. Cuddle now. / Cuddle now.

PAM: I'm not cuddling anyone. Is that clear little boy?

BOY: Be my Granny. Please.

PAM: No. Bugger off.

The BOY exits. PAM is on her own.

A fuck would have been better.

PAM strokes Shaggy.

DODDIE is on his own. He is holding a flower.

DODDIE: Love me. Love me not. Love me. Love me not. Fuck. Fuck. Fuck.

The BOY enters.

BOY: Hello handsome.

DODDIE: Oh hello.

The BOY sits beside DODDIE.

BOY: Can I put my arm round you?

DODDIE: Sure.

BOY: Is that nice.

DODDIE: I think so yes.

BOY: I think you're perfect / fella.

DODDIE: What?

BOY: I think you're perfect.

DODDIE: What makes you think that?

BOY: I just have a feeling.

DODDIE: I am not perfect.

BOY: You are fucking perfect / to me.

DODDIE: You don't know me.

BOY: (*Hurt.*) Yeah, I do.

DODDIE: You don't.

BOY: It's been intense though. Don't you think it's been intense. / Like a proper relationship.

DODDIE: Right. I have issues.

BOY: I don't care.

DODDIE: I had a nervous breakdown.

BOY: I can help you work it / through.

DODDIE: Oh fuck off.

BOY: I can help you

DODDIE: How long ago was it?

BOY: What?

DODDIE: That your Mum died.

BOY: Seven years.

DODDIE: Your Dad?

BOY: Murdered.

DODDIE: Oh Jesus.

BOY: Brutally.

DODDIE: Fuck. What kind of cancer was it?

BOY: Breast. She died with no hair and no tits.

There is a pause.

Fuck I like you fella.

DODDIE: Please stop.

BOY: Stop what?

DODDIE: Stop saying it. / It's ridiculous.

BOY: I really fucking like you.

DODDIE: Please stop it.

BOY: I think I might be falling / for you.

DODDIE: Oh Jesus.

BOY: What is it?

DODDIE: I can't do this.

BOY: What?

DODDIE: I can't get intimate with you like this. I am sorry. It's just not appropriate.

BOY: I'm heartbroken.

The BOY touches DODDIE's face gently.

DODDIE: You're going to have to go. I have huge intimacy issues.

BOY: I fucking love you.

DODDIE: Stop.

BOY: Will you be my family?

DODDIE: I can't… I…

BOY: Please.

DODDIE: I'm better on my own…

BOY: Please. I don't want to be on my own anymore. I LOVE YOU.

PETER is on his own. He is stroking Shaggy. PETER looks at Shaggy.

PETER: Is this what life has come to.

He continues stroking Shaggy.

I loved you once. I truly loved you.

BOY: Who did you love?

PETER: Fuck. You made me jump.

BOY: Who did you love?

PETER: None of your business.

BOY: Who did you love?

PETER: I loved my wife.

BOY: You don't love her anymore?

PETER: I'm not answering that question. I don't know. You're too young.

BOY: How can you not love your wife?

PETER: You're not Welsh. She'll be disappointed you're not Welsh.

BOY: Sorry mate.

The BOY goes and sits beside PETER. The BOY picks up the car magazine.

You like cars old man?

PETER: Yes. I like cars. Don't be cheeky.

BOY: I like big engines.

The BOY rubs his crotch. PETER does nothing.

Do you like big engines?

PETER: What?

BOY: Do you like big engines?

PETER: Oh I know your type.

BOY: What?

PETER: I was in the army. I know your type.

BOY: What you talking about?

PETER: Plenty of queers in the army.

BOY: Queers?

PETER: Poofters?

BOY: So?

PETER: I didn't mind them. I don't mind the poofters. But I'm not one of them.

The BOY continues to rub his crotch.

BOY: You don't want it?

PETER: (*Gently.*) No. I don't want it.

The BOY stops.

They were all rubbing themselves in the trenches.

BOY: Cool.

PETER: No shortage of penises in the trenches.

BOY: Sweet.

PETER: Please leave little boy. You're being very, very inappropriate.

BOY: I ain't little.

PETER: (*Firm.*) Leave now. I won't take this any further. I won't.

BOY: Alright. Keep your hair on.

PETER: Please.

BOY: Nice pants by the way.

PETER: Sorry?

BOY: The ladies' knickers. Fucking lovely.

PETER: Oh yes. Thanks.

BOY: I'd love to get you hard in those. (*Looking in the suitcase.*)
You have lots of pairs?

PETER: Yes. A collection.

The BOY lifts out a pair of pink pants.

Those are my favourite.

BOY: Hot, they feel hot.

PETER: Twenty per cent silk. Marks and Spencers. Expensive.

There is a pause. They look at each other.

That pink would suit your colouring. Pink always suits a
fair skin.

They look at each other again.

BOY: You're great fella.

PETER: Oh stop.

BOY: I think I might be falling for you.

PETER: Don't be ridiculous.

*The BOY approaches PETER. They are both in their underwear. The
BOY kisses PETER.*

BOY: Can I borrow your car magazine?

PETER: You can keep it. As a present.

BOY: Cheers old man.

PETER: Go on now. Back to your family.

BOY: Will you be my Grandpa?

PETER: No.

BOY: Please.

PETER: I don't know you.

BOY: Doesn't matter I don't mind. You could just pretend.
Please Grandpa. Help me.

PETER: I don't think so. I am not up to it, anymore. Off you go
now.

*The BOY is now on his own. He takes the picture of MARTIN out
of his pocket.*

SCRATCHIT is on her own.

SCRATCHIT: I don't feel dried up. Not nice to be your own.
The loneliness is palpable. FUCK. CUNT. FUCK.

The BOY enters.

BOY: Hello.

SCRATCHIT: Hello.

BOY: How's it going?

SCRATCHIT: Oh. You know. Hanging in there. Back again?

BOY: Yep.

SCRATCHIT: Nice to see you.

BOY: Really?

SCRATCHIT: Yes. You're a surprise.

BOY: A surprise?

SCRATCHIT: Yes.

BOY: Like Christmas.

SCRATCHIT: I suppose. Yes.

BOY: I like your caravan the best.

SCRATCHIT: It's very dirty.

BOY: But cosy.

SCRATCHIT: Sorry.

BOY: A caravan is cosy. You feel safe.

SCRATCHIT: I don't often feel safe. I'm all bruised.

BOY: Right.

SCRATCHIT: My vagina is all bruised.

BOY: Shall I kiss it better?

SCRATCHIT: Certainly not. It's one of the symptoms.

BOY: Are you sick?

SCRATCHIT: I don't know.

BOY: You make me hard.

SCRATCHIT: No I don't.

BOY: You're a sexy bitch.

SCRATCHIT: That is enough. I'm not having this. You're too young. It's totally unacceptable. Get out.

BOY: You don't know what your missing Missus.

SCRATCHIT: Mizz. I'm Mizz. Not Mrs.

BOY: Whatever. Missus.

SCRATCHIT: Go on. Fuck off.

BOY: So no pussy action then?

SCRATCHIT: That's right. No pussy action. You're too young. / Bugger off.

BOY: My father was murdered.

SCRATCHIT: Oh dear.

BOY: Brutally.

SCRATCHIT: I'm sorry.

BOY: Do you feel sorry for me?

SCRATCHIT: No. But I do have sympathy little boy.

BOY: I ain't little. You any brothers or sisters.

SCRATCHIT: One brother. You?

BOY: Only child.

SCRATCHIT: Were you spoilt?

BOY: I was in a home.

SCRATCHIT: That must have been nice.

BOY: Not really.

SCRATCHIT: Abused?

BOY: Oh yes.

SCRATCHIT: Jesus.

BOY: All the time.

SCRATCHIT: We were all abused.

BOY: Yes.

SCRATCHIT: My brother is a mongol.

BOY: Right. I know.

SCRATCHIT: You know?

BOY: I stole a photograph.

SCRATCHIT: Of Martin?

BOY: That's his name?

SCRATCHIT: Yes.

BOY: I thought he looked a bit weird.

SCRATCHIT: You naughty little thief.

BOY: I don't know any better do I?

SCRATCHIT: Suppose not.

BOY: Life of crime.

SCRATCHIT: You're funny.

BOY: So are you beautiful.

SCRATCHIT: Stop.

BOY: Beautiful.

SCRATCHIT: I'm not.

BOY: The beautiful girl.

SCRATCHIT: You mean that.

BOY: I don't know anything else.

SCRATCHIT: Thank you. My mother won't see Martin. Our family is fucked. I wish I had a brother like you.

BOY: I'll be your adopted brother.

SCRATCHIT: That's nice.

BOY: Would you like that?

SCRATCHIT: Yes.

BOY: I'd like that. I'd like it a lot. A sister. / A family.

SCRATCHIT: I would quite like a cuddle now. Can I have a cuddle?

BOY: Yes.

SCRATCHIT: You have to cuddle me.

BOY: What?

SCRATCHIT: You have to make the first move. You have to come and cuddle me.

BOY: Alright keep your hair on.

The BOY approaches SCRATCHIT. He cuddles her. SCRATCHIT is upset.

Do you want get fucked now.

SCRATCHIT: No. Just cuddled.

BOY: Not better to get fucked?

SCRATCHIT: No. Cuddled.

BOY: Right.

They cuddle again.

SCRATCHIT: Thank you.

BOY: For what?

SCRATCHIT: It's nice to be touched. I never get touched.

BOY: Would you like one kiss?

SCRATCHIT: Why not.

They stand looking at each other.

You have to make the first move.

The BOY approaches SCRATCHIT. He kisses her gently.

What a lovely boy you are.

BOY: This is much better than the home.

The BOY and SCRATCHIT hold each other. Tender.

SCRATCHIT: Bye, baby bunting,
Daddy's gone a-hunting,
To get a little rabbit skin
To wrap the baby bunting in.

To wrap the baby bunting in.
The rabbit skin. The rabbit skin. To wrap the baby
bunting in.

PETER and PAM are in the toilet cubicle of their caravan.

We hear moaning.

PETER is sick. PAM and PETER exit the caravan.

PAM: It's typical, just as we get going, you turn blue.

PETER: Well. You don't want me dying on you.

PAM: I don't know. Sometimes I wonder.

I love Shaggy.

PETER: Martin sent you a letter.

PAM: Who?

PETER: Martin. Your son. He sent you a letter.

PAM: Not another of those awful drawings.

PETER: Yes Pam. Would you like to see it?

PAM: What's it of?

PETER: See it and find out. I think it's rather good.

PETER pulls out a drawing from his tracksuit bottoms. He unfolds it.

It's his best picture yet.

PETER shows the picture to PAM.

PAM: What is it?

PETER: Can't you tell?

PAM: No. It just looks stupid.

PETER: It's a heart Pam.

Pause. PAM looks at the picture.

PAM: Useless.

PETER: He has written on the back. 'Dear Mummy. I love you'.

PAM: He has spelt love wrong.

PETER: Jesus Pam.

Short pause.

Are you happy that you incarcerated our son?

PAM: Yes.

PETER: You think you did the right thing?

PAM: Yes I do.

PETER: And you think he is happy?

PAM: As happy as he can be. Yes.

PETER: What does that mean?

PAM: I am never very sure how happy the mentally disabled are.

PETER: Out of the two, he's the child I'm most proud of.

PAM: He's certainly the least trouble.

PETER: Not long left.

PAM: What.

PETER: They don't live long Pam.

There is a pause. PETER looks at PAM.

There is a knock on the caravan door. DODDIE and SCRATCHIT enter the caravan.

PAM: Welcome to the 'New Hampshire' with the American-Style fridge / and built-in ice maker.

PETER: Oh Jesus.

Pause.

DODDIE: Is Shaggy / alright?

PAM: Very healthy. Thanks for asking.

DODDIE: Does Shaggy do tricks?

PETER: Oh / yes.

DODDIE: What kind of tricks does / Shaggy do?

PAM: I told your Father about the vaginal atrophy. No man is going to want you / now. With a dry fanny.

PETER: When did you last see Shaggy?

DODDIE: I saw him in a bucket.

PETER: Was he running around.

DODDIE: No. He wasn't running around. He was / in a bucket.

SCRATCHIT: There is no built in ice-maker.

PAM: Don't be so bitter.

PETER: Shaggy can get quite frisky you know.

DODDIE: Frisky?

PETER: Shaggy is a bit of a dark horse.

DODDIE: (*Still confused.*) Right. / Dark horse. Yes.

PAM: Where the fucking hell was my Shaggy?

DODDIE: He was sat a yellow bucket.

PAM: Well I wonder who left him / there?
  Was he lively?

DODDIE: / No.

PAM: This early menopause is a terrible, / disappointment.

SCRATCHIT: Right.

PAM: And you seem to be growing a moustache.
  Your father went blue today.

SCRATCHIT: Right. Dad?

PAM: I was a bit suicidal last Wednesday, Joan had her leg amputated, Rosemary has / colon cancer.

DODDIE: You sure Shaggy / is alright?

PETER: It's inedible Pamela.

PAM: Sorry?

PETER: The dinner. / It's inedible.

PAM: Inedible?

PETER: Yes. / What is it?

PAM: I mixed them / together.

SCRATCHIT: What?

PAM: The curry / and the stew.

SCRATCHIT: /Right.

PETER: What did you do / that for?

PAM: Curry or stew? / Curry or stew?

SCRATCHIT: Why didn't you just give us / one or the other.

PAM: I didn't feel like it. / Curry or Stew?

SCRATCHIT: Right.

PAM: I felt like mixing them / both together.

SCRATCHIT: It's / revolting.

PAM: None of you gave me an answer. Curry or stew. Curry or stew.

SCRATCHIT: You could / have chosen.

PAM: Why should I have / to chose?
It's not difficult?
You could have been nice?

PAM: Why? Curry or stew. Curry or stew.

SCRATCHIT: It's not a difficult / decision to make.

PAM: Why I deserve a decision. / That much I deserve.

SCRATCHIT: Just be nice Mum. / JUST BE NICE.

PAM: WHY? One doesn't / need to be nice.

DODDIE: You're like a small cunting child.

PAM: Hold on a wee minute. You little bastard. You can't speak to me like that.

DODDIE stares at PAM.

PAM: PETER. WOULD YOU DO SOMETHING. / NOW. DO IT NOW.

SCRATCHIT: I am having the early menopause. / Please stop shouting.

PAM: Oh fuck you. You self-obsessed little bitch.

PAM slaps SCRATCHIT. SCRATCHIT says nothing. There is a pause.

Change Shaggy's nappy.

PETER says nothing.

Change Shaggy's nappy.

PETER says nothing.

Now Peter. Change the FUCKING nappy now.

PETER: No.

PAM: No?

PETER: No.

PAM: No? What kind of an answer / is that?

PETER: No. Shaggy is dead / Pam.

PAM: Dead?

PETER: Dead Pam. Shaggy has been stuffed. Shaggy doesn't need to go to the FUCKING toilet.

PAM: Stuffed?

PETER: Yes. Is your son stuffed?

PAM: What?

The BOY arrives on his bike. There is a pause. He is holding the photograph that he took from the caravan. SCRATCHIT takes the photograph.

SCRATCHIT: Martin?

PAM: What about Martin?

SCRATCHIT: At least Martin didn't judge.

PAM: Martin didn't know how to fucking judge.

SCRATCHIT: Jesus Mum. That's the most honest thing I have heard you say in years.

SCRATCHIT approaches her Mother. She points her finger in her face.

Go and deal with Martin. You know he's dying. You loved a fucking stuffed dog. Take the fucking photograph.

Nothing. PETER is looking at the drawing.

PAM: I see a beam of intense darkness.

PAM approaches the BOY with the knife.

The lights snap to black.

THE END.

LOBSTER

Characters

TOBIAS
CHATTY
BOY

Folie à deux *(literally, 'a madness shared by two')* *is a rare psychiatric syndrome in which a symptom of psychosis (particularly a paranoid or delusional belief) is transmitted from one individual to another. The same syndrome shared by more than two people may be called* folie à trois, folie à quatre, folie à famille *or even* folie à plusieurs *(madness of many).*

The play is set in a concrete nuclear bunker. There is an aquarium with three lobsters in it.

An old lady enters (CHATTY), she dances to some music in an old fashioned manner.

A man enters. In his thirties. He has very pale skin. His hands are bandaged. They have been bleeding.

The old lady (CHATTY), moves towards the boy (TOBIAS), she stands in front of the boy for some time. CHATTY takes her hand gently down TOBIAS's cheek. Tender. There is a long pause.

CHATTY pinches TOBIAS's cheek. Like he is a small child. TOBIAS backs away from her.

CHATTY: What's wrong?

TOBIAS: Nothing.

CHATTY: You recoiled.

TOBIAS: Sorry.

CHATTY: Don't do that. Back off from Nan. Cruel.

TOBIAS: Sorry Nan. Sorry.

CHATTY: You're getting big.

TOBIAS: Do you think?

CHATTY: Fucking enormous. Did you grow in the night?

TOBIAS: Not sure.

CHATTY: You have taken on inches.

TOBIAS: Really?

CHATTY: Must be all that protein.

TOBIAS: Makes you grow.

CHATTY: That's right my boy. Shall we measure / you?

TOBIAS: Why not.

CHATTY: Oh yes.

TOBIAS: Yes?

CHATTY: You are really shooting up. / A big boy.

TOBIAS: Am I a man?

CHATTY: Nearly.

TOBIAS: / I feel like a man.

CHATTY: You're shooting up.

TOBIAS: I feel strong. Like a large hunting dog.

CHATTY: Ready for the kill.

TOBIAS: / Yes.

CHATTY: Good boy.

TOBIAS: Ready for the kill.

CHATTY: Are you on tippy toes?

TOBIAS: No.

CHATTY: No cheating. Do it properly.

TOBIAS: Yes Nan.

CHATTY: Look at you. You're growing up.

CHATTY marks TOBIAS's height.

At least two inches.

TOBIAS: Since yesterday?

CHATTY: Yes. Amazing.

TOBIAS: Life must be working.

CHATTY: It must.

TOBIAS: If I'm growing so much. The boy is becoming a man. / I have hair on my chin.

CHATTY: Yes. Sleep well?

TOBIAS: When?

CHATTY: In the night?

TOBIAS: God no. Sweating. / Awful.

CHATTY: Between the legs?

TOBIAS: Always.

CHATTY: My turn.

CHATTY stands by the wall. TOBIAS measures her.

Well?

TOBIAS: Bad news.

CHATTY: Oh yes.

TOBIAS: Still the same.

CHATTY: Bugger. / No movement.

TOBIAS: No movement.

TOBIAS: None.

CHATTY: / No growth.

TOBIAS: No growth.

CHATTY: / Must be dying.

TOBIAS: Must be dying.

TOBIAS: Shit.

CHATTY: / It's very disappointing.

TOBIAS: It's very disappointing.

CHATTY: / Very, very disappointing.

TOBIAS: Very, very disappointing.

TOBIAS: Yes very.

CHATTY: But you're a big boy.

TOBIAS: Yes. / Huge.

CHATTY: A big handsome boy.

TOBIAS: I'm a big handsome boy.
   Can I see the pyramids?

CHATTY: You certainly can my boy.

TOBIAS: The Great Pyramid of Giza. Amazing.

CHATTY: Would you like to go?

TOBIAS: Oh Nan. I dream about it.

CHATTY: Well you can't.

TOBIAS: Please Nan.

CHATTY: We are not made of money you know.

TOBIAS: Sorry Nan. Maybe one day?

CHATTY: Maybe.

TOBIAS: I could have a cappuccino?

CHATTY: They don't have cappuccinos in Egypt.

TOBIAS: Oh.

CHATTY: They only have cappuccinos in Italy.

TOBIAS: Right. Yes. Well fuck Egypt let's go to Italy. We could
   see the Pope.

CHATTY: I think he might have died.

TOBIAS: That's sad.

CHATTY: I saw it on the news. 'Pope Dead Shocker'.

TOBIAS: Poor Bastard.

CHATTY: Terrible looking funeral. Very poor looking coffin, if you ask me.

TOBIAS: No money.

CHATTY: People have given up with religion.

TOBIAS: Not surprising. All those stabbing, murders, and muggings. Out there, in the world. It's not surprising. Nan? Have you ever seen anything nice?

CHATTY: Not really.

TOBIAS: Shame.

CHATTY: Oh I did see one thing.

TOBIAS: Oh yes?

CHATTY: I saw a mongol doing some recycling.

TOBIAS: (*Unsure.*) Right.

CHATTY: There he was. Sat in amongst the outdoor madness with all these boxes filled with plastic and glass, and paper.

TOBIAS: Oh yes.

CHATTY: In amongst the pillaging, he was sorting, putting all the plastic in one box, all the glass in the other, and all the paper in another box. So sweet. Such a simple act, in amongst such chaos. Sweet little mongol.

TOBIAS: Saving the environment.

There is a pause. CHATTY is smiling. TOBIAS looks baffled.

CHATTY: Oh. Sorry. I didn't tell you the most important bit.

TOBIAS: Oh yes.

CHATTY: Every time he picked up a piece of glass. He kissed it.

TOBIAS: Not the plastic?

CHATTY: No. Like the glass was his small friend.

TOBIAS: Awwww.

CHATTY: Nice little boy. Innocence among the madness.

TOBIAS: Did you give him some money?

CHATTY: No.

TOBIAS: You should have.

CHATTY: You think?

TOBIAS: Yes. He could have bought himself lots of lollies.

CHATTY: He's probably dead. The mongols don't live long.

TOBIAS: Maybe the Pope's not dead?

CHATTY: Maybe.

TOBIAS: Because we don't know. Do we?

CHATTY: We don't know what?

TOBIAS: What's fact. What's fiction.

CHATTY: That's right my boy.

TOBIAS: Propaganda.

CHATTY: Oh that's terrible.

TOBIAS: Maybe they were lying about the Pope.

CHATTY: Oh that's terrible.

TOBIAS: Maybe he's not dead at all. They just tell us what we need to hear.

CHATTY: Oh that's terrible.

TOBIAS: I saw something nice.

CHATTY: Oh that's terrible.

TOBIAS: Nan!

CHATTY: Sorry son. What did you say?

TOBIAS: I said. I said. I saw something nice

CHATTY: Oh yes. Where on earth would you have seen something nice?

TOBIAS: I have my ways. I have an imagination. I function.

CHATTY: Oh yes. You function?

TOBIAS: Yes I function. My imagination functions.

CHATTY: Oh yes.

TOBIAS: In my dreams.

CHATTY: Oh yes. Here we go again.

TOBIAS: I was on my own.

CHATTY: Oh yes. Not with me.

TOBIAS: No. Not with you.

CHATTY: Oh yes. In your dream?

TOBIAS: Yes. In my dream. I was all alone. Except for little people.

CHATTY: Little boys and girls?

TOBIAS: Yes.

CHATTY: Boys.

TOBIAS: No. Not boys. They had hair on their chins.

CHATTY: What?

TOBIAS: Does that mean they're men?

CHATTY: How small?

TOBIAS: Smaller than you.

CHATTY: Jesus. How revolting.

TOBIAS: Were they men?

CHATTY: What were they doing?

TOBIAS: Well. None of them would talk to me.

CHATTY: How rude.

TOBIAS: They had hair on their chins, hundreds of little people. All on roller coasters.

CHATTY: Well, only children would be on roller coasters.

TOBIAS: It looked rather good fun to me.

CHATTY: Fun?

TOBIAS: Yes. Fun. But not one of them would talk to me.

CHATTY: Did you like that?

TOBIAS: No. I wanted to be their best friend. And there was one little red house, which I climbed into. I wanted to join in. But no-one would let me. I felt stuck. Alone.

CHATTY: And did you want me?

TOBIAS: Yes. It was strange. I had this pang in my stomach.

CHATTY: Where's Granny?

TOBIAS: Yes. Where's Granny.

CHATTY: You needed me to look after you.

TOBIAS: I think so. I just felt stuck.

CHATTY: And the little red house?

TOBIAS: A man. Who was not a man.

CHATTY: I don't understand.

TOBIAS: He was a man. But not dressed as a man.

CHATTY: Oh dear. How dirty.

TOBIAS: He was dressed like a lady.

CHATTY: This is ridiculous.

TOBIAS: No it's fucking not. I saw him. Clear as day. A man. But dressed as a pretty lady. A pretty lady with hair on his chin. I asked him a question. Do you want to know what I asked him?

CHATTY: No. Not really.

TOBIAS: Nan. This is serious. Ask me?

CHATTY: Ask you what.

TOBIAS: Take an interest. Take in an interest in me. I'm haunted. The small people. The roller coasters. The man. The man, that was not a man. Is that me?

CHATTY: How would I know?

TOBIAS: I asked him. I asked him if I was a man.

CHATTY: Oh yes.

TOBIAS: He said I was. He told me not to be afraid. He said I was a hound. / A male hound.

CHATTY: A hound.

TOBIAS: Yes. A male / hound.

CHATTY: / What is this nonsense?

TOBIAS: The man told me.

CHATTY: / In the dream.

TOBIAS: Yes in the dream.
The man. That was not a man. He told me. I'm the master.

CHATTY: This is shit.

TOBIAS taps the glass of the aquarium once again, with his bandaged hands.

TOBIAS: Should I be afraid. Eh? Little Lobster?

He taps the glass once again.

Should the hound be / afraid.

CHATTY: Jessie is catfood.

TOBIAS: What?

CHATTY: Jessie is catfood.

TOBIAS: Right. Yes

CHATTY: Kiss. Now.

TOBIAS: Now?

CHATTY: Yes, now.

TOBIAS: Not later?

CHATTY: Nope. Now.

> *TOBIAS approaches CHATTY. He kisses her on the cheek.*

No Tobias. Not right. Again. You know the score.

> *TOBIAS kisses CHATTY again, it is very inappropriate. The kiss of lovers.*

Good boy.

TOBIAS: Better now?

CHATTY: Yes. Much.

TOBIAS: I love you Nan.

CHATTY: You too. Stay?

TOBIAS: Yes.

CHATTY: Always?

TOBIAS: Yes. Goes without saying.

CHATTY: Good boy. Much better than the world.

> *TOBIAS taps the glass of the aquarium three times with his bandaged hands.*

TOBIAS: HELLO! Are you alright in there.

CHATTY: Leave Jessie.

TOBIAS: Are you bearing up? Under the strain?

CHATTY: Under the strain?

TOBIAS: I just / wondered?

CHATTY: What the fuck?

TOBIAS: If the lobster was bearing up?

CHATTY: Jessie is a lobster.

TOBIAS: And?

CHATTY: I'm not sure they feel the strain.

TOBIAS: Oh. I am sure they do.

CHATTY: How can a lobster bear up under the strain?

TOBIAS: Listen. I know about these creatures. I know things.

CHATTY: Cocks.

TOBIAS: Sorry?

CHATTY: Cocks. Boy lobsters are called cocks. And the girl
    lobsters are called hens.

TOBIAS: Cocks and hens.

*TOBIAS goes to the shelf. He takes one of the white cartons from it.
He takes a measuring pipette out of his pocket.*

Shot?

CHATTY: Eh?

TOBIAS: Shot. Shot of Gina?

CHATTY: Gina?

TOBIAS: / G.

CHATTY: Oh, love the G. / Breakfast?

TOBIAS: Yes, why not.

CHATTY: Why not.

TOBIAS: One ml?

CHATTY: Does nothing now.

TOBIAS: One point five.

CHATTY: Ah why not. / You're addicted.

TOBIAS: So are you.

CHATTY: Better than nothing. Love the Gina G.

TOBIAS measures the G out of the container into two small glasses. He fill them with juice.

TOBIAS: / Down the hatch.

CHATTY: Down the hatch.

They both drink.

TOBIAS: Horrible.

CHATTY: They are sophisticated creatures.

TOBIAS: Sophisticated?

CHATTY: Their nervous systems. They have autonomic nervous systems.

TOBIAS: Eh?

CHATTY: They know when dangers is coming.

TOBIAS: Fuck.

CHATTY: They go into shock when harmed.

TOBIAS: (*Tapping the glass.*) Are you in shock little cock?

CHATTY: Would you like to know something very sweet?

TOBIAS: About Jessie?

CHATTY: Yes. About Jessie.

TOBIAS: Oh yes please Nan.

CHATTY: If Jessie was to have a child. She would be able to hold its baby's hand.

TOBIAS: Claw to Claw.

CHATTY: Pincer to Pincer. The have great social skills.

TOBIAS: Fuck.

CHATTY: Give me your hand.

TOBIAS holds out his hand. CHATTY takes it.

TOBIAS: Who am I?

CHATTY: You're the baby lobster.

TOBIAS: And I am the baby.

CHATTY: And I am holding your hand.

TOBIAS: It's nice.

CHATTY: Not sore?

TOBIAS: A bit sore. But you are protecting me.

CHATTY: That's right.

TOBIAS: By the simple act of holding my hand.

CHATTY: You have to destroy their nervous systems, before you kill them.

TOBIAS: And their brains?

CHATTY: Their brains are all the same. Across the board. Exact replicas.

TOBIAS: Across the board. Like our brains. / Just like our brains.

CHATTY: Just like our brains.

TOBIAS: / Just like our brains.

CHATTY: Just like our brains

TOBIAS: / We think the same.

CHATTY: We think the same.

TOBIAS: / And do the same.

CHATTY: And do the same.

TOBIAS: / And feel the same.

CHATTY: And feel the same.

CHATTY: Just like those two lobsters. Sadly our legs can't grow back.

TOBIAS: Eh?

CHATTY: Lobsters. If they lose a leg. It will grow back.

TOBIAS: Super.

CHATTY: And their eyes, or claws or antennae.

TOBIAS: Amazing. I fucking love those lobsters.

Pause.

Nan?

CHATTY: Yes?

TOBIAS: Did you know that you have two black eyes?

CHATTY: Yes.

TOBIAS: How?

CHATTY: Smack the Granny. Punch the Granny.

TOBIAS: But I didn't hit / you.

CHATTY: Punch the Granny.

TOBIAS: How did you get the two black eyes Nan?

CHATTY: Boys came.

TOBIAS: No they didn't.

CHATTY: They did, they bloody did. In the night. Very frightening. / Let me tell you.

TOBIAS: No they didn't.

CHATTY: They did. They quietly crept in wearing boxing gloves.

TOBIAS: Nan. Stop. Did you / hit yourself?

CHATTY: Smack the Granny. Punch the Granny. / Smack the Granny. Punch the Granny.

TOBIAS: Did the boy hit you?

CHATTY: Maybe. / Maybe not.

TOBIAS: Tell me. Tell me now. Did he hit you?

CHATTY: Who wants / to know.

TOBIAS: Nan. Tell me the fucking truth.
DID YOU HIT YOURSELF?

CHATTY: I thought it right. Yes. What choice did / I actually
have?

TOBIAS: With the boxing gloves?

CHATTY: Always.

TOBIAS: Nan!

*CHATTY stares into space, distracted. We hear music. TOBIAS is
playing with something inside his mouth. Blood drips down the side
of his mouth onto his shirt. He pulls out a tooth.*

Fuck.

CHATTY says nothing.

Nan?

CHATTY: Yes.

TOBIAS: I don't like this.

CHATTY: What?

TOBIAS: I feel stuck.

CHATTY: Stuck.

TOBIAS: Yes. In myself.

CHATTY: Unhappy?

TOBIAS: I think so.

CHATTY: It happens more and more.

TOBIAS: Is it the end?

CHATTY: No it's just the beginning.

TOBIAS: The beginning of what?

CHATTY: You're growing.

TOBIAS: / Yes.

CHATTY: A big handsome boy.

TOBIAS: Yes. Nan. I'm so worried.

CHATTY: Stop this.

TOBIAS: What happens next. Is this it?

CHATTY: It's not so bad.

TOBIAS: Will I end up in the little red house?

CHATTY: Better to stick with what we know.

TOBIAS: / Yes.

CHATTY: What we are comfortable with.

TOBIAS: But the little men?

CHATTY: Stop this.

TOBIAS: What will happen to the little men?

There is a pause.

Nan?

CHATTY: Yes?

TOBIAS: Every day I think I am dying.

CHATTY: I know my boy.

TOBIAS: Terrible.

CHATTY: Terrible. Yes.

TOBIAS: Really awful. A life of anxiety.

CHATTY: It's all about death.

TOBIAS: I'm scared.

CHATTY: I know you are my boy.

TOBIAS: Scared of the dying.

CHATTY: Really.

TOBIAS: To think I had some sort of existence.

CHATTY: Really?

TOBIAS: Yes. I like to think I went to school. Lived a little. Fuck. Fuck. Fuck. This is a fucking nightmare.

There is a silence. The silence is unbearable.

CHATTY: Keep talking.

TOBIAS: Yes.

CHATTY: The silence I can't deal with. / You know that.

TOBIAS: I'm very stuck.

CHATTY: Talk. You know what happens in the silences. / Ask me something?

TOBIAS: You get scared.

CHATTY: Yes.

TOBIAS: In silence you fear / things most.

CHATTY: Ask me something. Quick. The fear is setting in.

TOBIAS: I don't…

CHATTY: NOW TOBIAS. The silences I can't deal with. Never been silent. Have we my boy?

TOBIAS: No Nan.

CHATTY: Fill the silence Tobias. Fill the silence. Think.

TOBIAS: Holiday?

CHATTY: Yes. Holiday. Marvellous. We haven't had that / for ages.

TOBIAS: Holiday.

CHATTY: Form the question.

TOBIAS: Right. Yes.

There is a pause. TOBIAS is stuck.

CHATTY: Form the question.

TOBIAS does nothing.

TOBIAS: Holiday. I…

CHATTY: I am warning you. / FORM THE QUESTION.

TOBIAS: JESUS FUCK. JESUS FUCK. Holiday…I…What…
Fuck…

CHATTY: It's not much to ask. Is it?

TOBIAS: No.

CHATTY: Do it. Or pay. Form the question Tobias.

TOBIAS: Holiday. Holiday. Holiday.

CHATTY: WHERE WAS MY FAVOURITE HOLIDAY
DESTINATION?

TOBIAS: Yes! That's it. That's it. Where was your favourite
holiday destination? It was on the tip of the tongue.

CHATTY: Now. Do it now. Form the question properly.

TOBIAS: Hello Nan.

CHATTY: Hello.

TOBIAS: Hello.

TOBIAS: Can I ask you a question?

CHATTY: Yes. That would be lovely.

TOBIAS: OK. Here goes. Nan?

CHATTY: Yes.

TOBIAS: Where was your favourite holiday destination?

CHATTY: Auschwitz.

TOBIAS: Ah?

CHATTY: Do you know where that is.

TOBIAS: Well, considering I have never been anywhere. That seems like a redundant question.

CHATTY: Stupid fuck. It's in Poland.

TOBIAS: Ah?

CHATTY: And do you know who worked there?

TOBIAS: No.

CHATTY: Your Grandfather. Tobias?

TOBIAS: Oh yes I remember now.

CHATTY: And didn't he do a super job?

TOBIAS: Yes Nan.

CHATTY: Do you love your planes.

TOBIAS: Yes Nan.

CHATTY: Super German soldier. Absolutely super. Super job. How many time did you wash your hands today?

TOBIAS: One hundred and three.

CHATTY: Oh dear.

CHATTY pinches TOBIAS's cheek. Like he is small child.

TOBIAS: Stop that.

CHATTY: Hands bleeding?

TOBIAS: Always yes. You know that. They are always bleeding. It is a constant.

CHATTY: Constant?

TOBIAS: Yes. The bleeding hands are a constant in my life. The pain. The blood.

CHATTY: You're being weird.

TOBIAS: No I'm not.

CHATTY: Constant? What kind of word is that to use.

TOBIAS: The man dressed as the pretty lady / used it.

CHATTY: Stop this.

TOBIAS: He did. He said that pain was a 'constant'. / In the dream.

CHATTY: Stop using that stupid word.

TOBIAS looks at his bandaged hands.

Bleeding hands.

TOBIAS: Pathetic isn't it?

CHATTY: Sore?

TOBIAS: Yes. Very.

CHATTY: Oh lovely. Oh super. Let me see.

TOBIAS: Right. You sure you want to see?

CHATTY: Yes.

TOBIAS: It's not pleasant.

CHATTY: I went through childbirth.

TOBIAS: You don't think it's cruel?

CHATTY: No I don't.

TOBIAS: I'm going to make them bleed more. Will you like that?

CHATTY: Oh yes.

TOBIAS: Scratch the sores. Self harm.

CHATTY: Self harm?

TOBIAS: Yes. I'm going to self harm.

CHATTY: Self harm? Self harm?

TOBIAS: Yes. And you think that's fine.

CHATTY: Of course I do.

TOBIAS: And what if I was to cut my hand right off.

CHATTY: Just for fun.

TOBIAS: No. Not for fun. For you.

CHATTY: Right.

TOBIAS: I would cut my hand off for you.

CHATTY: What a gesture.

TOBIAS: It wouldn't grow back Nan.

CHATTY: Nope. It wouldn't. Although it would be an amazing gesture.

TOBIAS: Better off without it?

CHATTY: Maybe?

TOBIAS: It's cruel. Do you agree?

CHATTY: Yes I agree. But the world is cruel my boy.

TOBIAS: I don't live in the world.

CHATTY: You live here.

TOBIAS: That's right. I live here. I could take a knife right now. And just cut through the skin, and bone, and cartilage.

CHATTY: That is your choice.

TOBIAS: It is. It is my choice. Life is cruel. So you say. So why should I not experience some of that?

CHATTY: Stop this. You're here. You're safe.

TOBIAS: I don't feel safe.

CHATTY: No?

TOBIAS: No. I don't feel safe.

CHATTY: But you have me?

TOBIAS: I feel alone.

CHATTY: But I'm here.

TOBIAS: Do you want to know something?

CHATTY: Are you going to cut your hand off now?

TOBIAS: Maybe. I feel more lonely when I'm with you.

CHATTY: You're just having an episode. A drama. You're being weird.

TOBIAS: Maybe I should cut both my hands off?

CHATTY: Maybe.

TOBIAS: And my legs.

CHATTY: Oh yes. What a statement. Shall I get the knife.

TOBIAS: Why not.

CHATTY goes to a drawer. She takes a carving knife out of it. She hands it to TOBIAS.

Maybe my head should go first?

TOBIAS raises the knife to his neck.

CHATTY: Aren't you funny.

TOBIAS: I want to cut my head off. Get rid of it. Cut the fucking thing off.

TOBIAS takes the bandages off, they are in a very bad state.

Happy now?

CHATTY: Sorry.

TOBIAS: What do you see?

CHATTY: Your beautiful hands.

TOBIAS: No Nan. What do you see?

CHATTY: A lovely boy / that I am so proud of.

TOBIAS: No Nan what do you see?

TOBIAS puts his hands very close to CHATTY's face.

Come on Nan. What do you see?

CHATTY: Blood.

TOBIAS: Any why do you see blood

CHATTY: You're frightening me.

TOBIAS: I just want an answer. A decent, / honest answer.

CHATTY: What about some jam roly poly?

TOBIAS: Why do you see blood?

CHATTY: With custard?

TOBIAS: ANSWER ME!

CHATTY: Poor frail old woman. Being tortured.

TOBIAS: Answer the question.

CHATTY: Because you wash your fucking hands too much.

TOBIAS: Yes Nan. Go on. And why?

CHATTY: I…

TOBIAS: Come on Nan. Why do I wash my hands?

CHATTY: Because you think everything you touch…I…

TOBIAS: Yes. Go on.

CHATTY: Because you think everything you touch. You will die.

TOBIAS: Good. We are getting somewhere. / Progress.

CHATTY: What is this?

TOBIAS: It's a conversation Nan.

CHATTY: Ah.

TOBIAS: We are having a conversation. You are helping.

CHATTY: It's fucking boring.

TOBIAS: Right. I'm cutting my head off.

He takes the knife to his neck again.

Tobias is cutting his head off. Off it goes.

CHATTY: NO. WAIT! STOP THIS. What do you want from me?

TOBIAS: Sorry?

CHATTY: What do you want from me?

TOBIAS: I just want to know one thing?

TOBIAS says nothing.

CHATTY: Come on you stupid boy. What is it then?

TOBIAS: Fuck. I…

CHATTY: You should think yourself lucky. There was a queen.

TOBIAS: Yes.

CHATTY: Her name was Mary.

TOBIAS: Right.

CHATTY: She had her head cut off.

TOBIAS: Lucky her.

CHATTY: And she had a Jack Russell terrier called Skye.

TOBIAS: Did she cut it off herself?

CHATTY: No. She was punished. And she had a Jack Russell terrier. And the man who cut her head off. He tried to make the Jack Russell terrier, drink the blood of the Queen. His mummy. And do you know what. The Jack Russell terrier didn't touch the blood.

TOBIAS: What happened to the Jack Russell terrier?

CHATTY: The Jack Russell terrier went to its mummy's bed.

TOBIAS: To sleep?

CHATTY: To die.

TOBIAS: Fuck. That's sad. The poor Jack Russell terrier.

CHATTY: It is.

TOBIAS: The Jack Russell terrier was heartbroken. The Jack Russell terrier had lost his mother. And the Jack Russell terrier could no longer exist.

CHATTY: Yep. So just have a little think about your own life.

There is a pause. CHATTY lifts the knife. She kisses the blade.

TOBIAS: Will it snow? When you die. I love the snow. I could make a snowman.

There is a pause.

CHATTY: You've never seen the snow.

TOBIAS says nothing.

Tobias? Have you ever seen the snow?

TOBIAS: Yes.

CHATTY: (*Warns.*) Tobias.

TOBIAS: No.

CHATTY: That's right. It's all lies.

TOBIAS: Yes.

CHATTY: All made up.

TOBIAS: Yes. What choice did I have.

CHATTY: Would you like to be a fireman when you grow up?

TOBIAS: No. Not a fireman.

CHATTY: A Doctor?

TOBIAS: No not a Doctor.

CHATTY: I know. I know.

TOBIAS: Yes?

CHATTY: An astronaut!

TOBIAS: No. Not an astronaut.

CHATTY: A racing car driver?

TOBIAS: No wrong again. A hunter.

CHATTY: A what?

TOBIAS: I would like to be hunter.

CHATTY: To kill things.

TOBIAS: Yes. Too kill things.

CHATTY: Where's the light Tobias?

TOBIAS: There's the light.

CHATTY: Where's the light?

TOBIAS: There's the light.

CHATTY: Where's the light?

TOBIAS: There's the light.

CHATTY: Where's the light?

TOBIAS: There's the light.

CHATTY: Where's the light?

TOBIAS: There's the light.

CHATTY: Where's the light?

TOBIAS: Please stop.

CHATTY: Where is the light?

TOBIAS: Stop now.

CHATTY: Where. Is. The. Light?

TOBIAS: Please. I can't.

CHATTY: WHERE IS THE FUCKING LIGHT Tobias?

CHATTY kicks TOBIAS in the balls.

TOBIAS: There. Is. The. Light. Nan.

CHATTY: Good boy.

TOBIAS: I want to punch you now.

CHATTY: Do you have a whiff of it?

TOBIAS: I have a whiff of it.

CHATTY: Right in the middle of the phizzog. Hard. Hit me.

TOBIAS: No. It's cruel.

CHATTY: Come on. Hit me hard.

TOBIAS: Stop.

CHATTY: Make the old nose bleed. Hit it hard. See the blood dripping down.

TOBIAS: I am not hitting you today.

CHATTY: The last time was super. Absolutely super. You had the gold ring on. You got me right between the eyes.

TOBIAS: Shut up. Fucking shut up.

CHATTY: The blood poured down. What a sight it was. That lovely metallic taste. Don't be such a jessie. Punch me.

TOBIAS: Nan. Stop.

CHATTY: / Hit me.

TOBIAS: Please.

CHATTY: / Come on fuck me. Fuck me. Punch me. Fuck me. Punch me.

TOBIAS: / I love you. I love you. I love you.

CHATTY: Love the Nan. Punch the Nan. Fuck the Granny. Punch the Granny. Fuck the Granny. Punch the Granny. Tell me to take my knickers off.

TOBIAS: Take your knickers off.

CHATTY: Why?

TOBIAS: You just asked me to.

CHATTY: Take my knickers off.

TOBIAS: Take your knickers off.

CHATTY: Take my knickers off.

TOBIAS: Just take your knickers off.

> *CHATTY removes her pants from under her skirt.*

Good girl.

CHATTY: Punch me now.

TOBIAS: This is stupid. / Fucking stupid.

CHATTY: Come on you big poof. Punch me. Punch the Granny.

> *TOBIAS raises his fist. There is a silence. TOBIAS looks very uncomfortable, and anxious. CHATTY closes her eyes.*

The excitement is palpable.

TOBIAS: Palpable?

CHATTY: Yes. Palpable. I feel the excitement is palpable.

TOBIAS: I can't.

CHATTY: Do it Batty Boy.

TOBIAS: (*Warns.*) Nan.

CHATTY: Chutney ferret.

TOBIAS: Stop.

CHATTY: Jobby jabber.

TOBIAS: Please.

CHATTY: Come on. Fucking knob jockey.

TOBIAS: Jesus.

CHATTY: Back door bandit. Cock knocker. DONUT PUNCHER. Punch the fucking Granny.

> *TOBIAS raises his fist. There is a pause.*

TOBIAS: The hunter is hunting. Hunting the kill.

CHATTY: You'll be lucky. It's your birthday tomorrow.

TOBIAS: Is it?

CHATTY: Yes.

TOBIAS: How exciting. How old will I be?

CHATTY: I don't know.

TOBIAS: I want to know.

CHATTY: I can't answer that.

TOBIAS: Why? I want to know. Please tell me. Please.

CHATTY: I have amnesia.

TOBIAS: Tell me Nan.

CHATTY: Just fuck up Tobias.

CHATTY exits. TOBIAS is left alone.

There is a pause.

TOBIAS approaches the lobster aquarium.

TOBIAS: (*Sings.*)
Baa Baa Black Sheep, have you any wool.
Yes Sir, Yes Sir, three bags full.
One for the master, and one for the dame.
And one for the little boy. Who cried down the lane.

A BOY enters with CHATTY. He has a gag on.

CHATTY: (*Sings.*)
The wheels on the bus go round and round.
Round and round.
Round and round.
The wheels on the bus go round and round.
All day long.

TOBIAS: What the fuck have you brought that out for?

CHATTY: I thought it might be fun.

TOBIAS: Oh really?

CHATTY: Yes. / Really.

TOBIAS: Put him back Nan.

CHATTY: He's my new dancing partner. / Isn't he super?

TOBIAS: Put him back. I don't want to look at / him. I…

CHATTY: Let's ask him some questions.

CHATTY undoes the BOY's gag.

TOBIAS takes the BOY's arm. His face is covered in vomit.

BOY: Blanket.

TOBIAS: Sorry?

BOY: Blanket.

CHATTY: Blanket? Blanket?

BOY: Can I have a blanket.

CHATTY: Blanket?

BOY: Yes…I'm cold. Can I have a blanket.

CHATTY: Blanket. Blanket. Blanket.

CHATTY makes a farting noise.

TOBIAS: Yes you can have a blanket. You're cold. So you can have a blanket.

TOBIAS exits. CHATTY approaches the boy. He is now lying down. CHATTY puts the rubber stopper of her walker into the boys mouth.

CHATTY: Good boy. You're a good boy. Does it taste good?

The BOY says nothing.

Answer the question son. What does it taste of?

BOY: Rubber? The walker tastes of rubber?

CHATTY: Rubber? Rubber? It tastes of rubber?

BOY: Yes it tastes of rubber.

CHATTY: Does it taste good?

BOY: Yes. It tastes good.

CHATTY makes a farting noise.

TOBIAS returns with the blanket and a cloth. He puts the blanket over the BOY.

Thank you.

TOBIAS: My pleasure.

The BOY is lying on the ground. We hear him shivering.

BOY: I don't feel well. Sorry Miss Chatty.

CHATTY: You are not going to have one of those funny turns are you?

BOY: I feel quite ill. I think… Sorry Miss Chatty.

CHATTY: Oh Jesus, Mary, Joseph and the Donkey. Here we go again.

The BOY goes into spasm. He is having a fit.

CHATTY and TOBIAS continue watching the boy. He is writhing on the floor.

TOBIAS: He might choke.

CHATTY: Yes. He might.

TOBIAS: Choke to death.

CHATTY: Yes. Might be a blessing in disguise.

The BOY continues to fit. TOBIAS and CHATTY watch. The BOY stops. He stares at TOBIAS and CHATTY.

TOBIAS: / Alright now?

CHATTY: Alright now?

TOBIAS: / All over?

CHATTY: All over?

TOBIAS: / Alright now?

CHATTY: Alright now?

BOY: Yes. Sorry Miss Chatty.

CHATTY: They don't stop?

BOY: No. They don't stop.

CHATTY: They're a pain in my arse.

BOY: Sorry. Sorry / Miss Chatty.

CHATTY: A big pain in my arse.

BOY: Right. Yes. Sorry Miss Chatty.

CHATTY: Sick of watching you.

BOY: Please could I have a glass of water.

CHATTY: HOW THE FUCK DID YOU GET HERE?

BOY: You drugged me and brought me here.

CHATTY: Drugged DRUGGED? NO I DIDN'T. HOW DID YOU GET HERE? GET THE FUCK OUT. GET OUT OF MY HOUSE.

CHATTY grabs the BOY's neck. The BOY screams.

TOBIAS: Stop. Stop this now.

TOBIAS pulls CHATTY off the boy.

CHATTY: HE IS TRYING TO TAKE YOU AWAY FROM ME. HE IS TRYING TO TAKE YOU AWAY.

TOBIAS: Stop this Nan. Stop it. You're going to hurt him.

CHATTY: HURT HIM? I DON'T FUCKING CARE.

TOBIAS holds CHATTY's face in his hands.

TOBIAS: Now listen. From now on. No more hurting. No more.

CHATTY: Yes. I just got scared. That is all. I thought you were leaving me.

TOBIAS: I am not going anywhere. I am here.

CHATTY: Do you still love me?

TOBIAS: Yes Nan. Of course.

CHATTY: I get scared. I thought…

TOBIAS: I'm not going anywhere.

CHATTY: Are you not grateful?

TOBIAS: Of course I am.

CHATTY: For all I have done for you?

TOBIAS: Nan. I am not going.

CHATTY: You would leave an old woman?

TOBIAS: I'm not leaving.

CHATTY: Promise?

TOBIAS: Promise.

CHATTY: The same brain.

TOBIAS: The same brain.

CHATTY: Just like lobster.

TOBIAS: Just like lobster.

> *CHATTY goes to exit. She turns to TOBIAS.*

Leave the boy?

CHATTY: Yes. Leave the boy. And put me to bed. Tuck me in.

TOBIAS: Is he safe?

CHATTY: Doors closed. All fine. Come with?

> *CHATTY stops at the door. She turns to the BOY.*

Your mother?

BOY: What?

CHATTY: Where is your mother?

BOY: Dead.

CHATTY: Your Father?

BOY: Dead.

CHATTY: You're an orphan?

BOY: Yes Miss Chatty.

CHATTY: A sweet little orphan.

BOY: Yes Miss Chatty.

CHATTY: You see we did you a fucking favour.

BOY: Yes Miss Chatty.

CHATTY: Am I your Mummy?

BOY: Yes Miss Chatty.

CHATTY: Must be very sad. To be all alone in the world. Isn't it lucky that you now have us. Right I'm going for a slash.

CHATTY exits with TOBIAS. The BOY is left alone. He looks lost. He stands for sometime. The BOY has another fit.

TOBIAS enters. He watches the BOY who is now lying on the floor.

BOY: I had another one.

TOBIAS: Right. What do you think about?

BOY: When?

TOBIAS: During the fits.

BOY: Nothing. Blank.

TOBIAS: That must be nice.

There is a silence. The BOY sits up. TOBIAS looks at the BOY, tenderly. He then takes his hand and strokes the BOY's cheek.

BOY: She is getting worse.

TOBIAS: She is not. / Leave her out of it.

BOY: She is. She is getting sick Tobias.

TOBIAS: Leave it. She is fucking / fine.

BOY: She is losing it.

TOBIAS: STOP FUCKING SLAGGING / MY NAN!

BOY: Alright. / Calm down.

TOBIAS: WELL FUCKING STOP IT. STOP FUCKING SLAGGING HER. SHE IS MY NAN. MY NAN.

There is a pause.

BOY: I would like a cigarette.

TOBIAS: Twenty pence.

BOY: What?

TOBIAS: That's the going rate. For a cigarette.

BOY: Jesus.

TOBIAS: Leave him out of it.

BOY: Are you serious?

TOBIAS: Slag my Nan, you can pay twenty pence. Stupid cunt.

BOY: My wallet.

TOBIAS takes the wallet, out of the BOY's pocket.

TOBIAS: You know the deal.

BOY: Yes. Take it.

TOBIAS: No need for attitude.

BOY: I wasn't…

TOBIAS: NO NEED FOR FUCKING ATTITUDE.

BOY: Sorry. Take the money.

TOBIAS: Twenty pence. That's the going rate. Right, I am now going to take twenty pence from your wallet.

BOY: Yes. Good. Take it. Whatever.

TOBIAS: Whatever?

BOY: Yes. Whatever. TAKE THE MONEY.

TOBIAS takes the twenty pence. He kisses it.

TOBIAS: Worth every penny. Eh? Next time without the attitude please.

TOBIAS takes a packet of cigarettes out his pocket, and gives the BOY one. He lights the cigarette with a match.

BOY: Fuck that's good.

TOBIAS: You were left alone with my Nan?

BOY: Yes.

TOBIAS: Are you alright?

BOY: Yes.

TOBIAS: Nan. She didn't hurt you?

BOY: No. She made me taste her walker.

TOBIAS: She's a rough old bird. Did it taste good?

BOY: What do you reckon?

Pause.

TOBIAS: Oh. I found some help for you.

BOY: Sorry?

TOBIAS: Some help. Hostage help. Help for hostages. Try and make you feel better.

BOY: Right. Yes.

TOBIAS: (*Interrupting.*) Just listen. Important advice.

TOBIAS takes a piece of paper out of his pocket.

He reads.

Right. What do you do if you are taken hostage? Number one, be patient, time is on your side. Avoid drastic action. Number two. Do not speak unless spoken too, and only when necessary. Do not talk down to the captor who may be in agitated state. I'm not agitated, what are they talking about, agitated? Avoid appearing hostile. DO NOT look the captor directly in the eye. Well I'm not so sure about that one. Treat the captor like royalty. Oh, yes, I like that one. Attempt to establish a rapport with the captor. If medication, first aid, or restroom privileges are needed by anyone – say so. The captor in all probability does not want to harm persons held by him or her. IF THE CAPTOR TRIES TO COVER YOUR HEAD WITH A BAG, SACK, OR OTHER OBJECT, IT HAS NOW BECOME NECESSARY FOR YOU TO FAKE AN ILLNESS OR FAINT. Does that help?

Pause.

BOY: I don't get this?

TOBIAS: I'm fucking helping. Trying to lift your spirits. I am trying to help you. Now listen. Attempt to establish rapport with the captor. If medication, first aid, or restroom privileges. SAY SO. Do you need to go to the restroom?

There is a pause.

Do you need to go to the rest room?

BOY: Restroom?

TOBIAS: Yes. Do you wish to go to the restroom?

BOY: I don't know.

TOBIAS: You don't know? / You don't know?

BOY: Yes. / I don't know.

TOBIAS: You don't know if you need to go to the restroom?

BOY: Yes.

TOBIAS: I'm trying to make you feel / better.

BOY: Right. But I don't know what a restroom is?

TOBIAS: I AM / TRYING.

BOY: Yes, I know.

TOBIAS: This is difficult for me too you know. I'm finding this very tricky. This situation.

BOY: Tricky?

TOBIAS: Yes. Tricky. It's a tricky situation. I have feelings. / I hold feelings.

BOY: For what?

TOBIAS: For you. I hold feelings for you. Do you need to go to the restroom?

BOY: I'm sorry. / I don't know...

TOBIAS: Toilet. Toilet. Do you need to go to the fucking toilet?

BOY: No.

TOBIAS: Right. Good. Progress. Handsome.

BOY: Sorry?

TOBIAS: You're handsome.

BOY: Thank you.

TOBIAS: Am I handsome?

BOY: I don't know.

TOBIAS: You don't know.

BOY: Yes.

TOBIAS: It's a simple question. Am I handsome?

BOY: I'm not sure.

TOBIAS: Right. That's disappointing.

BOY: What is?

TOBIAS: That you don't know.

BOY: It seems strange.

TOBIAS: That a boy's handsome?

BOY: That boys ask that of other boys.

TOBIAS: I want to know.

BOY: Right.

TOBIAS: You never answer the question.

BOY: What do you want me to say?

TOBIAS: I want you to tell me the truth. Do you think I am handsome?

BOY: Right. I don't know. I just don't know.

TOBIAS: Fuck.

BOY: What.

TOBIAS: You're not right for me?

BOY: Well maybe you should find someone else?

TOBIAS: No.

BOY: Maybe I'm not right?

TOBIAS: No. You are.

BOY: Other boys might be better?

TOBIAS: No. Nan is right. Nan is always right. / She will make you right.

BOY: Oh Jesus.

TOBIAS: There is no need for that.

BOY: Well. It's exasperating.

TOBIAS: Fuck you.

BOY: I am not going to give you what you want.

TOBIAS: You fucking are.

BOY: I'm not. / I'm not up to it.

TOBIAS: You will. We will make you.

BOY: I won't do it. / I have had enough.

TOBIAS: You ungrateful little cunt.

BOY: I don't care Tobias. Do what you like. I don't care. I won't give you it.

TOBIAS slaps the BOY.

It doesn't even hurt. It's pathetic.

TOBIAS: You see?

BOY: What?

TOBIAS: I'm a man. Only a man would hit another man, isn't that right?

BOY: Not necessarily.

TOBIAS: I am the hunter. And you are the hunted.
Do you think I'm handsome?

BOY: Oh Jesus. / I don't know Tobias.

TOBIAS: Do you feel anything?

BOY: For what?

TOBIAS: For us.

BOY: I feel a loyalty towards you.

TOBIAS: Loyalty?

BOY: Yes. It's strange. Yes. I feel a loyalty towards you both. I feel like a small baby.

TOBIAS: A baby?

BOY: Its sounds odd. Yes. But I feel like I'm the / baby and you're my parents.

TOBIAS: We feed you?

BOY: Yes.

TOBIAS: We put you in the bath?

BOY: Yes.

TOBIAS: We buy you clothes?

BOY: Yes.

TOBIAS: We play with you?

BOY: Yes.

TOBIAS: I'm the Daddy, and Nan's the Mummy.

BOY: That's right.

TOBIAS: And you're the tiny little boy?

BOY: Yes.

> *There is a pause. TOBIAS touches the BOY's face.*

You're my Daddy.

TOBIAS: And Nan?

BOY: She is my Mummy.

TOBIAS: And you are a baby?

BOY: Well, kind of. Yes. I have formed an attachment to you both.

TOBIAS: I'm the man in this relationship.

BOY: Relationship.

TOBIAS: Yes. We are having a relationship.

BOY: A close relationship?

TOBIAS: Yes. It's close

BOY: Yes Tobias.

TOBIAS: Are you happy?

BOY: I don't know?

TOBIAS: It is a very simple question.

BOY: It's been too long now.

TOBIAS: How long now?

BOY: Sorry?

TOBIAS: How long have you been here now?

BOY: About four and a half months I think.

TOBIAS: It's my birthday tomorrow.

BOY: How old will you be?

TOBIAS: I don't know. Nan won't tell me.

BOY: How old do you think you are?

TOBIAS: Am I younger than you?

BOY: No.

TOBIAS: Are you a boy.

BOY: No.

TOBIAS: That means I'm actually a man.

BOY: You're probably about thirty Tobias.

TOBIAS: Fuck.

BOY: Is that a shock?

TOBIAS: Yes. I think so.

Pause. The BOY smiles.

We don't feel sorry for you.

BOY: I don't want you to.

TOBIAS: We don't feel sorry for you. Even though I have
formed… We have formed… A close relationship…
I don't feel sorry for you.

BOY: Right. Yes.

TOBIAS: Nanny told me. She told me that we don't feel sorry
for you. We don't. You serve a purpose. That's all.

BOY: A purpose?

TOBIAS: Yes. You serve / a purpose.

BOY: I don't…?

TOBIAS: We are doing nothing wrong. We are just forming close relationships.

BOY: (*Confused.*) Right. O.K.

TOBIAS: Our brains told us. We have the same brain you see. Me and Nan.

BOY: Yep. I'm clear on that one.

TOBIAS: Tomorrow is my birthday.

BOY: That's right Tobias. Aren't you clever?

TOBIAS: Do you think?

BOY: Yes. I think, you're super smart.

TOBIAS: Thank you.

BOY: A very clever boy.

TOBIAS: Do you love us?

BOY: No.

TOBIAS: You will.

BOY: I won't.

TOBIAS: You will. Eventually. I am the Master. And I could cut your head off.

BOY: What?

TOBIAS: I won't but I could. Easily. But you will love me.

BOY: I won't.

The BOY slowly kisses TOBIAS.

Nice?

TOBIAS: Yes.

BOY: You want to fuck my ass.

TOBIAS: Yes.

BOY: You don't ever think about leaving?

TOBIAS: I go out all the time.

BOY: No you don't.

TOBIAS: Yes I do. I went and had a cappuccino yesterday.

BOY: Tobias, you have never been out.

TOBIAS: A small cappuccino. Delicious. NO chocolate though.

BOY: It's all in your head.

TOBIAS: Yes.

BOY: All made up.

TOBIAS: Yes. No cappuccinos.

BOY: Tobias's sad little life.

TOBIAS: Watch it.

BOY: Come out and have a cappuccino with me?

TOBIAS: No. Not unless Nan can come.

BOY: Just for a while. / See how we go.

TOBIAS: Nan would not be pleased.

BOY: We could knock her out.

TOBIAS: How?

BOY: Punch her up a bit?

TOBIAS: She loves that. I could hit her really hard.

BOY: Right in the middle of her face.

TOBIAS: Unconscious.

BOY: Yes. We could nip out for a bit.

TOBIAS: See the world.

BOY: You'd like that.

TOBIAS: Cars and lorries and / pyramids.

BOY: And big vans.

TOBIAS: And cappuccinos. And you wouldn't tell anyone?

BOY: About?

TOBIAS: About your life here. With me and Nan.

BOY: You are my life.

TOBIAS: That's right. Its been good fun, hasn't it.

The BOY kisses TOBIAS.

TOBIAS: I love that noise.

BOY: What noise?

TOBIAS: The noise of kissing. Fucking love it.

BOY: Let's go out tomorrow.

TOBIAS: For your birthday?

BOY: Yes.

TOBIAS: Punch Granny.

BOY: Punch Granny.

The BOY kisses TOBIAS. They kiss for some time.

CHATTY enters. She is carrying a rifle.

CHATTY: Yoo hoo. Yoo hoo. Anybody home?

BOY: Oh Jesus.

CHATTY: Hello. Hello. Anybody in the house?

BOY: Hello Chatty.

CHATTY: Who are you?

TOBIAS: Nan. Put the rifle down.

CHATTY: And who are you?

TOBIAS: Tobias.

CHATTY: Who are you people? What are you doing here. Get out. GET OUT.

TOBIAS: I'm your Grandson. Put the rifle down.

CHATTY: (*Sings.*)
   There was a young man from Belgrave
   Who kept a dead whore in a cave
   He said; I've got to admit
   I'm a bit of a shit,
   But think of the money I'll save.

   Did you speak?

BOY: No.

CHATTY: Yes you did. You spoke.

BOY: No I didn't.

CHATTY: I'll blow that disabled brain of yours out your head.

TOBIAS: Watch me Nan. Watch me.

CHATTY: Finger on the trigger. And it's all over.

TOBIAS: There was a young man from Belgrave.

CHATTY: Oh lovely.

TOBIAS: Who kept a dead whore in a cave.

CHATTY: Oh super.

TOBIAS: I've got to admit,
   I'm a bit of a shit,
   But think of the money I'll save.

CHATTY: (*Still pointing the gun at the BOY.*) Fucking marvellous. You?

BOY: Yes?

CHATTY: Punch me.

TOBIAS: Yeah. Go on. Punch the Granny.

BOY: Me?

TOBIAS: Yeah. You. Punch my Granny.

BOY: You said you were going to do it?

TOBIAS: No I didn't. NO I DIDN'T.

BOY: Yes you did.

TOBIAS: Oh no I didn't.

BOY: Yes you did. Yes you did.

TOBIAS: No I didn't.

CHATTY: COME ON YOU BIG POOFS. PUNCH ME.

BOY: FUCK.

TOBIAS: Knock her unconscious. As agreed.

BOY: Fuck. / Fuck, Fuck.

TOBIAS: Do it. Do it now. Come on. Punch her. She fucking loves it.

The BOY raises his fist. CHATTY closes her eyes.

CHATTY: PUNCH THE FUCKING GRANNY.

The stage goes to black.

We hear music.

Lights up. The next day.

TOBIAS enters. He looks at his hands. Then looks at the lobster. He uses one of his hands to impersonate the lobster.

TOBIAS: Look at you. With your big pincers. Amazing creature. The right is bigger than the left. Jessie. The right handed lobster. Maybe you're right handed. Just like your Daddy. If I don't eat will I die Jessie. If you get in a bath that's too hot, do you burn Jessie? Are eggs bad for babies Jessie. Does eating roly poly make you fat Jessie. If I cut my head off would it be a good thing, or a bad thing Jessie. Should I cut my head off now Jessie. I am my own person Jessie, I live in the world. Jessie. Jessie. Jessie.

CHATTY enters, she is now very black and blue. She carries several balloons filled with music.

We hear music. CHATTY dances with the balloons.

TOBIAS enters. He is wearing pyjamas.

Oh Hello Nan.

CHATTY: Hello son.

TOBIAS: You look terrible.

CHATTY: Thanks.

TOBIAS: All black and blue.

CHATTY: Yes.

TOBIAS: Really awful.

CHATTY: Not good?

TOBIAS: Not good.

CHATTY: Worse than before?

TOBIAS: Much worse. Up all night?

CHATTY: Yes. Sore face.

TOBIAS: Not surprising. All that punching.

CHATTY: You didn't hit me hard enough. I'm a tough old bird.

Pause.

TOBIAS: Why the balloons?

CHATTY: You don't remember?

TOBIAS: No.

CHATTY: (*Sings.*) Happy birthday to…

TOBIAS: Who?

CHATTY: You. Happy birthday to you.

TOBIAS: Ah.

CHATTY: Happy birthday dear Tobias.

TOBIAS: How old.

CHATTY: Happy birthday to you.

TOBIAS: How old am I Nan?

> *CHATTY makes a farting noise.*
>
> The boy says I'm about thirty.
>
> *CHATTY makes two farting noises.*
>
> NAN! If I'm about thirty. That means I'm a man.
>
> *CHATTY makes three farting noises.*
>
> How old are you Nan?

CHATTY: I am probably about a hundred and seven. Who the fuck knows.

> *Pause.*

TOBIAS: Pills.

CHATTY: Pills?

TOBIAS: They haven't kicked in.

CHATTY: Distracted?

TOBIAS: Yes. Very. Outside myself.
I feel I am outside myself. Not all here.

CHATTY: Poor creature.

TOBIAS: Impending doom.

CHATTY: Where?

TOBIAS: On its way.

CHATTY: Stomach?

TOBIAS: Bad. Churning.

CHATTY: Panic?

Pause.

TOBIAS: Fuck. Feel bad.

CHATTY: Worse than ever.

TOBIAS: Think so.

CHATTY: Gina G?

TOBIAS: Yes. Make me feel better. Level me out.

CHATTY: The boy?

TOBIAS: Sorry.

CHATTY: The boy?

TOBIAS: Ah. Sleeping. He looks sweet.

CHATTY: Who?

TOBIAS: The boy. When he's sleeping.

CHATTY: Well he's a pain in my arse while he's awake.

TOBIAS: Birthday present?

CHATTY: Sorry.

TOBIAS: You promised a birthday present?

CHATTY: Oh yes. No present.

TOBIAS: That's disappointing.

CHATTY: Wisdom instead.

TOBIAS: Right.

CHATTY: Are you ready. Wisdom for my special boy. Wisdom and advice. I'm old.

TOBIAS: Yes.

CHATTY: And you're young.

TOBIAS: I think so yes.

CHATTY: I have lived beyond my years.

TOBIAS: Yes Nan.

CHATTY: So I am giving you a foundation. Something to think about. When I die.

TOBIAS: Like the Queen's Jack Russell terrier?

CHATTY: Yes. Like the Jack Russell terrier.

CHATTY: There is much to be said for solitude. There is no drug that can save us from our solitude.

TOBIAS: Not even the Gina.

CHATTY: Not even the Gina. The Gina fucks us up. But if there was something…

TOBIAS: (*Interrupting.*) Is there something?

CHATTY: No my boy. Sadly there's not. And that is the reason the world doesn't work. We have nothing that makes life worth living.

TOBIAS: We have each other.

CHATTY: But I am an old fucker.

TOBIAS: Yes.

CHATTY: The boy won't do it. No-one will. There is nothing that makes life worth living but solitude. Because everything else is misery. Total abject misery. If there was I would let you out into the world.

TOBIAS: Really?

CHATTY: Yes. My boy.

TOBIAS: You either live with those that love you. Or you live alone in solitude.

CHATTY: You got it my boy.

TOBIAS: And you're not lying?

CHATTY: I have never lied to you.

TOBIAS: Right.

CHATTY: Do you believe me?

TOBIAS says nothing.

Pause.

TOBIAS: Who slept with you last night?

CHATTY: You did.

TOBIAS: No I didn't.

CHATTY: All that punching put you off?

TOBIAS: No.

CHATTY: Do I repulse you?

TOBIAS: What?

CHATTY: All that bruising. Enough to put a boy off.

Pause.

TOBIAS: Who slept with you last night?

CHATTY: You did. You always do.

TOBIAS: Well I didn't last night.

CHATTY: All that punching put you off?

TOBIAS: I slept with the boy.

CHATTY: Oh yes. Good luck with that.

TOBIAS: I spooned him.

CHATTY: You what?

TOBIAS: That's what the boy said. He called it spooning. He said I'm the big spoon and you're the little spoon. Can I spoon you.

CHATTY: Good luck with that.

TOBIAS: I felt close to him. Safe and warm.

CHATTY: I'll spoon you in a minute if you're not careful.

TOBIAS: I felt safe.

CHATTY: Romance.

TOBIAS: What.

CHATTY: It's called romance. You are being romantic.

TOBIAS: Right. / I liked it.

CHATTY: It doesn't last. It's transient.

TOBIAS: But I liked it.

CHATTY: Tobias. Romance never got us anywhere. It's another of those drugs that doesn't work.

TOBIAS: It's bad for you.

CHATTY: Yes. It will never make you happy.

There is a pause. TOBIAS looks at CHATTY.

TOBIAS: Is a hound a hound?

CHATTY: What?

TOBIAS: A hound. Is it actually a hound.

CHATTY: What kind of a stupid question is that.

TOBIAS: Just answer me.

CHATTY: Yes.

TOBIAS: And a lobster is a lobster?

CHATTY: Yes. What the hell else is it going to be.

TOBIAS: And a man is a man?

CHATTY: Yes. You're a weirdo.

TOBIAS: What about the man in the dream. He was not a man.

CHATTY: Yes he was.

TOBIAS: No he wasn't. He was something else.

CHATTY: A show off.

TOBIAS: Stop it. It's like he had tried something else. Tried to be something else.

CHATTY: Did he seem happy?

TOBIAS: Fuck no. He was miserable.

The BOY enters. He is wearing pyjama bottoms and nothing else.

BOY: Morning.

TOBIAS: Morning darling.

CHATTY: Oh Jesus. You have got to be joking. Darling? Darling? Go on piss off.

TOBIAS: Let him stay.

BOY: Yeah. Let me stay.

TOBIAS approaches the BOY. He kisses him.

CHATTY: This is fucking disgusting.

TOBIAS: Sleep well?

BOY: Like a baby.

CHATTY: What is this?

TOBIAS: You look very fresh Joshua.

BOY: Do I?

TOBIAS: Yeah. Better than ever. I'm lucky.

BOY: Me too.

CHATTY: Who the fuck is Joshua?

TOBIAS: He told me his name. He's my boyfriend.

CHATTY: This has gone too far. We didn't bring you here for this. Kiss me.

TOBIAS: / No.

CHATTY: Now. Kiss me now.

CHATTY: Kiss me Tobias.

TOBIAS: (*To the BOY.*) Do I have permission.

BOY: Yes you have permission.

CHATTY and TOBIAS kiss.

CHATTY: Like seeing Chatty getting snogged.

BOY: Yes Miss Chatty.

CHATTY: He loves me you know.

The BOY says nothing.

Nothing to say.

There is a long silence.

TOBIAS: Nope.

CHATTY: Run out.

TOBIAS: Yep.

They all sit in silence.

CHATTY: All over is it?

TOBIAS: Think so.

CHATTY: (*To the BOY.*) And you? Nothing?

BOY: Nothing.

CHATTY: Mind gone blank?

BOY: Yep. Blank.

CHATTY: Jesus.

They all sit in silence.

CHATTY: Pyramids?

TOBIAS: Nope

CHATTY: (*Desperate.*) Cappuccinos.

They all say nothing. The BOY is smiling.

I have something to tell you.

CHATTY: Oh yes.

TOBIAS: You ready.

CHATTY: Oh yes. I'm ready.

TOBIAS: I'm not a lobster.

CHATTY: What?

TOBIAS: I AM NOT A LOBSTER. STOP TREATING ME LIKE A LOBSTER.

CHATTY: I know you're not / a lobster.

TOBIAS: I am not a lobster.

CHATTY: Stop saying that. Stop it.

TOBIAS: I am not a lobster. I am not a lobster.

TOBIAS approaches one of the aquariums. He lifts one of the lobster out.

CHATTY: Put Jessie back. Right now.

TOBIAS: Do you know the most humane way to kill a lobster?

CHATTY: / Stop this.

TOBIAS: Not putting them in boiling water. Oh no. That's cruel you see. They feel pain. (*To CHATTY.*) You told me that. You see Nan. The only way to do it is to take a very sharp knife.

He takes the knife from the table.

BOY: Jesus.

TOBIAS: And you take the knife down the back of the lobster's neck. And once you do it once you want to do it again, and again, and again. You have the compulsion you see. To kill. Because once you are over the initial shock. Of the first kill. You want to keep on going. It doesn't mean anything. No more thrills.

CHATTY: You deceived me.

TOBIAS: No I did not.

CHATTY: You did. You lied.

TOBIAS: There is much to be said for deceit. Isn't there boy?

BOY: Yes.

TOBIAS: Deceit is one of the great virtues of the world.

They all stand looking at each other. TOBIAS has control. He looks calm.

I wonder which lobster is next? Any ideas? Boy?

BOY: No. Oh no. I have no ideas.

TOBIAS approaches the aquarium. He is still holding Jessie.

TOBIAS: What about you Jessie? / Should I kill you?

CHATTY: Yes. Go on. Kill Jessie.

TOBIAS: No not Jessie. Jessie has never done anything wrong. Jessie has never lied. But one lobster has got to go. Eenie meenie miny mo. Catch a lobster by its toe, if it squeals let it go. Eenie meenie miny… Nan? Do you have any ideas?

CHATTY: Fuck you.

TOBIAS: I know exactly which lobster is next.

TOBIAS approaches CHATTY and the BOY with the knife. The stage goes to black.

THE END.

Also by Russell Barr

Sisters, Such Devoted Sisters

A shocking and lonely crime emerges from Glasgow's underworld. It provides the underlying sadness in this funny and touching coming-of-age story.

Winner of the Carol Tambor Award for the best piece of theatre at the Edinburgh Fringe 2004, *Sisters, Such Devoted Sisters* has also enjoyed successful runs in London and New York.

ISBN 978-1-84002-567-5 • £7.99

'a rich stew of a show that has the steamy stench of a dark Jacobean comedy... hilarious, excoriating and intensely moving' *Guardian*

'riotously funny' *Daily Telegraph*

'deliciously bitchy... only one victim, not a city or a people, but the more impactful for it' *Financial Times* (four stars)

'sad, grotesque and beautiful' *The Scotsman* (four stars)

'a funny and shocking first-hand account of life as a Glasgow transvestite. Barr has a wicked way with words and a habit of puncturing his funniest riffs with bleak observations of brutality' *Scotland on Sunday*

'vivid and compelling' *Independent* (Critics' Choice)